What Shall This Man Do?

Watchman Nee

What Shall This Man Do?

TYNDALE HOUSE PUBLISHERS
Wheaton, Illinois
CHRISTIAN LITERATURE CRUSADE
Fort Washington, Pennsylvania

Library of Congress Catalog Card Number 77-083597
ISBN 8423-7910-X, paper
Copyright © Angus I. Kinnear.
First published in 1961.
American edition published in 1978
by Tyndale House Publishers, Inc.,
Wheaton, Illinois 60187,
by permission of Kingsway Publications, Ltd.,
Eastbourne, Sussex, England.
Printed in the United States of America.
Scripture quotations are from the Revised Version.

95   94   93   92   91   90
12 11 10 9 8

Contents

Preface

This digest of the spoken ministry of Mr. Watchman Nee (Nee To-sheng) of Foochow is compiled, as were two earlier books, from notes and translations for which I am once again indebted to a number of friends who heard him. The addresses were originally given at various times and in widely different circumstances in China and the West over the five-year period from 1938 to 1942, a period of, for those days, severe testing for the Church in China.

In publishing these messages in their present form, I think it well to introduce a word of caution. The matter, some of it fragmentary, that I have brought together in this collection was not all in this proximity originally, nor can it be regarded as in any sense complete. While I have used prayerfully what is available to me without conscious bias, the arrangement of the material is in part my own, and the book may of necessity omit some aspects of the themes treated that the author, were he accessible, would wish to provide. Moreover the unavoidable effect of editing is to make the studies appear more systematic than they were ever intended to be, and this in itself could be misleading. For, notwithstanding the appearance of design given to them, they remain essentially talks, and reflect the preacher's need to emphasize, and even sometimes to seem to overstate, his points in order to bring them home to his hearers.

On the subject of "system" in Christian teaching, the author may perhaps be allowed to express himself. Discussing, twenty years ago, one of his early writings in Chinese, Mr. Nee said: "Some years back I was very ill, and the doctors said I could only live a few months. In the face of this I felt burdened to write down in book form what the Lord had shown me on the subject of 'the spiritual man,' and thus to share with others the light I had been given. I did so and it was published, and the edition is now exhausted. It will not be reprinted. It was not that what I wrote was wrong, for as I read it now I can endorse it all. It was a very clear and complete setting forth of the truth. But just there lies its weakness. It is *too* good, and it is the illusion of perfectness about it that troubles me. The headings, the orderliness, the systematic way in which the subject is worked out, the logic of the argument—all are too perfect to be spiritual. They lend themselves too easily to a merely mental apprehension. When a man has read the book he ought not to have any questions left; they ought all to be answered!

"But God, I have discovered, does not do things that way, and much less does he let us do them. We human beings are not to produce 'perfect' books. The danger of such perfection is that a man can understand without the help of the Holy Spirit. But if God gives us books they will ever be broken fragments, not always clear or consistent or logical, lacking conclusions, and yet coming to us in life and ministering life to us. We cannot dissect divine facts and outline and systematize them. It is only the immature Christian who demands always to have intellectually satisfying conclusions. The Word of God itself has this fundamental character, that it speaks always and essentially to our spirit and to our life."

It will help readers of the following pages if they bear the above remarks in mind. To some this book may appear to attempt too much, and to raise more questions than it answers. May some part at least of its message nevertheless have this power to speak, as from God, to any of us whose ambition is to become more effectual servants of Jesus Christ.

ANGUS I. KINNEAR

London 1961

1
God's Skilled Craftsmen

The calling of God is a distinctive calling. In some degree at least, this statement is true of all whom he calls. Their commissioning is always personal; it never stops at being general—to all men. "It was the good pleasure of God," says Paul, "to reveal his Son in me."

Moreover its object is always precise; never merely haphazard or undefined. By this I mean that, when God commits to you or me a ministry, he does so not merely to occupy us in his service, but always to accomplish through each of us something definite towards the attaining of his goal. It is of course true that there is a general commission to his Church to "make disciples of all the nations"; but to any one of us, God's charge represents, and must always represent, a personal trust. He calls us to serve him in the sphere of his choice, whether to confront his people with some special aspect of the fullness of Christ, or in some other particular relation to the divine plan. To some degree at least, every ministry should be in that sense a specific ministry.

It follows from this that, since God does not call each of his servants to precisely identical tasks, neither does he use precisely identical means for their preparation. As the Lord of all operations, God retains the right to use particular forms of discipline or training, and often, too, the added test of suffering, as means to his end. For his goal is a ministry that is not merely common or general, but rather, one specially designed for the service of his people in a given hour. To the servant himself, such a ministry must become peculiarly his own—something to be specially expressed because specially experienced. It is personal because it is first-hand; and it cannot be escaped because, in so far as it directly relates to the purpose of God, that purpose itself demands that it be fulfilled.

Every Spirit-taught reader of the New Testament will have noticed something of this. In its pages we can, I think, recognize at least three such distinctive emphases in ministry, represented by the particular historic contributions of three leading apostles. These three men, while certainly having very much in common, nevertheless display, at certain points in the record, differences of emphasis sufficiently striking to suggest that something quite original was being committed by God to each of them. I allude, of course, to the special contributions of Peter, Paul, and John. In the New Testament it is, I suggest, possible to trace three lines of thought, expressed no doubt in varying measure by all the apostles, but specially defined and illustrated by the unique contributions of these three in particular.

It will be seen that the distinctiveness of their three ministries is in part chronological, each apostle bringing, in the course of the history, his own fresh and timely emphasis to the fore. Moreover, it is certainly never such as to set the three men apart from or in conflict with one another, for what each one has is not something opposed, but rather, complementary to what the others have got. And perhaps, too, the difference between them lies less in their ministry as a whole than in what is recorded of it for our instruction. Yet I think it can be shown that the Petrine, the Pauline, and the Johannine strands or themes running through the Scriptures indicate three main historic emphases given by God to his people for all time. All the many and diverse ministries of the New Testament—those for example of Philip and Barnabas, Silas and Apollos, Timothy and James—together with the countless more that should follow in history, contain in differing proportions the distinctive elements of these three. It will be well, therefore, if we seek to understand what God is saying to us through the experiences of these three typical men and this will be the aim of our present study.

"CASTING A NET INTO THE SEA"

We begin with Peter. It is generally held that Mark, in writing his Gospel, was placing on record what were in fact Peter's recollections of his Lord. Added to these we have Peter's own Epistles, and of course the incidents of his life recorded by the other evangelists in the four Gospels and the book of the Acts. These together form the special contribution of Peter. What, then, was his ministry? Well, his Epistles certainly indicate to us how widely representative it was of all that made up the work of an apostle; but in the narrative passages one thing perhaps stands out above others. It is the thing to which I think the Lord drew special attention when, in calling him to follow, he used the term "fishers of men." That was to be Peter's distinctive task, and the one that fell first to him. He was to bring men, urgently and in great numbers, into the Kingdom. Further on in the story Jesus reaffirmed this, when, at Caesarea Philippi, Peter had confessed him to be the Christ of God. The Lord would build his Church, and Peter might later be called to a pastoral ministry of "feeding his sheep" therein; but, in relation to that Church, Jesus' first words to him are: "I will give unto thee the keys of the kingdom of heaven."

A key implies, among other things, an entry, a beginning. You come in by a door, and you use a key for opening it, or for letting others in. In the outcome, Peter's ministry often issued in such a beginning of things, and his was in fact the first to do so. The Church in Jerusalem began when three thousand souls received his word, and the church in Caesarea began when, in his presence, the Holy Spirit fell on Cornelius and his household. Thus we may say that, when Peter stood up with the eleven, he opened the door to the Jews, and when later he preached Christ in that Roman home, he opened it again to the Gentiles. So although on neither occasion Peter was alone, for the commission extends always to others beside him, and although later on we find that Paul too was a man chosen of God to have a still wider ministry of the gospel among the Gentiles, yet in a true sense Peter was the pioneer. Historically he held the key and he opened the door. His task was to initiate something. He was ordained by God to make the beginnings.

The burden of Peter's message was salvation—a salvation not for its own sake, but always with a view to the Kingdom in fullness, and in relation to Jesus, its exalted King. Yet when first he preached the Kingdom it was inevitably to lay stress, not upon its other aspects, but upon the beginning. It was to emphasize the keys, and their function of introducing the Kingdom to men. It may be more than a coincidence that this was, as we have said, in keeping with the details of his own call. For Peter was called under circumstances quite different from

Paul, and even, as we shall see, from John. Since those circumstances are recorded for us in Scripture, we should not discount them as fortuitous. They are worthy of notice.

Peter, we are told, was called while engaged in the main skill of his trade, namely, "casting a net into the sea." That occupation seems (speaking figuratively) to have given character to his ministry throughout his life. He was to be first and foremost an evangelist: one who starts something by "taking men alive." By casting a net you draw in fish—all sorts of fish. That is Peter; and without for one moment forgetting the wider range of what he did and wrote, it is nevertheless true to say that the main emphasis of what is recorded of his active ministry is placed there.

"THEY WERE TENT-MAKERS"

We come next to Paul. He is a servant of the Lord, but he is a different one. No one would suggest that Paul did not preach the gospel. Of course he did. To have done otherwise would have been to repudiate the pioneer work of Peter and throw away the ground gained by him. Do not let us make the mistake of thinking there was some basic conflict between the ministries of these two men, or that the ministries of God's servants should ever be in conflict. Paul makes it clear, in writing to the Galatians, that such differences as there were related to geography and race, and that in essence their tasks were complementary, not only by mutual consent, but in their value to and attestation by God (Gal. 2:7-12).

But the point is that there came a day when Paul was required to go further. Whereas Peter initiated things, Paul's task was to construct. God entrusted to him in a special way the work of building his Church, or in other words, the task of presenting Christ in his fullness to men, and of bringing those men *as one* into all that God had in his mind for them in Christ. Paul had glimpsed that heavenly reality in all its greatness, and his commission was to build together the gathered people of God, according to that reality.

Let me illustrate. You recall the vision that was granted to Peter before he set out to go to the Gentiles in Caesarea. He saw a sheet coming down out of heaven, held by the four corners and containing every kind of beast, clean and unclean. That vision signified the inclusive and universal intention of the gospel. It is directed *to every creature*. And that, again, is Peter first and foremost. His ministry is a ministry with a sheet—or a net, if you like—putting something of everything into it. It is God-ordained, for it comes to him "out of heaven." His commission from God, renewed and interpreted here at Joppa, was to bring as many as possible of every kind to the Savior.

But our brother Paul is different in this, that he is not a man holding a sheet; he is a tent-maker. The sheet of Peter's vision—again I speak figuratively—becomes in Paul's hand a tent. What do I mean? I mean this, that a sheet is something as yet without form; it is not yet "made up" into anything. But now Paul comes onto the scene as a tent-maker, and under the direction of the Spirit of God—under the constraint of a vision that, equally with Peter's, came to him out of heaven (2 Cor. 12:2-4; Eph. 3:2-10)—he gives that formless "sheet" a form and a meaning. He becomes, by God's sovereign grace, a builder of the House of God.

With Paul, it is not now a question merely of so many souls saved, but of something taking a definite form. It is probable that Paul never experienced anything like three thousand souls believing in one day. That was Peter's privilege, but the special ministry of Paul was to build believing souls together according to the heavenly vision which God had given him. God is not satisfied for his people merely to become converts, "going to church," sitting and hearing well-composed sermons, and feeling content that as a result they are good Christians. He is not even greatly interested in their special experiences of "second blessing," "sanctification," "deliverance" (or whatever terms they use)—*as experiences.* There is something more in the mind of God for his children even than these—something in terms of a "new Man" from heaven. God has in view, as his goal and object in redemption, the union of Christ the Head and the Church his Body, so that the whole, Christ *and* his Church, make up together his one new Man—"the Christ."

It is good to look through the Scriptures to find "*the* Christ." How blessed it is that the one thought in the mind of God is his Son, Jesus Christ! Many times in Scripture it is "Jesus the Christ," and many times again it is simply "the Christ." But look carefully and you will find that, not only is the term used of the Son of God personally, but it is used too so as to embrace others with him. (See especially 1 Cor. 12:12.) What measureless grace! God is securing for himself many redeemed sons, not just as individuals but as one gathered people. And with what object? To make of them, in the Son and with him, one new Man—one united whole wherein is expressed, through all those human lives, the heavenliness and the life and the glory of the blessed Sons of God.

That is God's tremendous object; and Paul was one called of God in a special way to be the steward of that mystery, both to set it forth and to bring his people into it. In saying this we do not mean in the least to belittle the ministry of Peter. We do not imply that evangelism should ever have less than its full place. But what we all need to see is this, that the special ministry of Paul is the necessary complement of that of Peter. Paul goes beyond Peter, but not to Peter's destruction or discredit. Even brother Peter, with all his own growing understanding of God's "spiritual house" (1 Peter 2:1-9), recognized that in some degree Paul had out-distanced him in this. It is very good to read the closing verses of his last Epistle, in which he refers to "the wisdom" given to Paul, and then goes on to class Paul's writings along with "the other scriptures." It may have needed grace to do that; but Peter had come to the place where he saw that, in the plan of God, the teaching of Paul had been truly complementary to his own.

"Woe is me," said Paul, "if I preach not the gospel"; and he sought the help of God to carry it to the farthest limits of the Roman world. But wherever he preached, it was not to stop with the first effect of the preaching but also to follow it through to its further purpose in the saints. For he was essentially a builder. Indeed, as he himself put it, he was a "masterbuilder" (1 Cor. 3:10). He laid the foundation—yes, the foundation of Jesus Christ—and then he went further and built on that foundation. To attempt to build on any other foundation would, he insisted, totally disqualify him. But even with that settled, he saw that the character of the building matters too. It matters greatly how you build, and with what materials. There can be no shoddy workmanship in God's house, no substitutes. God would have his people bonded together in love, framed and builded into a holy temple in the Lord and fitted to reveal and display the glories of his Son. That was the goal which Paul, by his ministry, set before us all. All the lessons of his eventful life, and all the rich contribution of his many writings, covering as they do so wide a range of time and space and action, have this one end in view: that Christ might have for himself the glorious Church for which he died.

"MENDING THEIR NETS"

But at the last there came set-backs and disappointments. In his letter to the Philippians, Paul tells us why. "All seek their own," he says, "not the things of Jesus Christ" (Phil. 2:21). Writing a little later to Timothy, he says of the saints in one Roman province that "all they of Asia" have turned away. Who are these Asian believers? Some of those, surely, whom the Lord himself challenges in his Apocalypse. Seven representative churches in the province of Asia are there addressed, because in their spiritual state they are typical, we believe, of the churches throughout the whole of this age (Rev. 1:11). For already, in the eyes of God, all the churches of that first New Testament period seem to have departed from his standard and missed something of the divine purpose.

At this point God calls in John. Till now, so far at least as the written New Testament record goes, he has remained in the background. But with Paul gone, the Lord now brings to light his further vessel of ministry, and with him a fresh distinctive emphasis to meet a new need.

The ministry of John is quite different from that of Peter. John was not personally or uniquely commissioned, as was Peter, to originate something. So far as our record tells us, the Lord only used him at the beginning *alongside* Peter. Nor is he shown to have been entrusted in any distinctive way with the task of making known the mystery of the Church. No doubt he was as concerned as were the other apostles in its foundation (Eph. 2:20), but in this too his calling was in no sense unique. Doctrinally he has nothing to add to the revelation given through Paul. In Paul's ministry the things of God reach a

climax, an absolute, and you cannot improve on
that. Paul's concern is with the full realization of
divine counsels that had been formed in the
Godhead before the foundation of the world.
Those counsels in his Son—that plan for man's
redemption and glory—God had caused to be
unfolded age by age, glimpse by glimpse, until at
last, in this special age of grace, it was made
fully manifest in the birth and death, resurrection and exaltation, of his Christ. The presentation of that plan in its wholeness, and the bringing of it to full realization in the people of God,
was Paul's special burden. His task was to express, for the benefit of us all, something coming
out of the very heart of God—something from the
eternities, now brought to light in time. To improve, therefore, on what God entrusted to Paul,
you would have to improve on God, and that is
inconceivable. The divine plan is absolute.

Then why to Paul add John? What need is
there for this further ministry? The answer is
that, at the end of the New Testament period, the
enemy of souls found entry into the house of
God, and caused God's own people, the very
heirs of redemption themselves, to turn aside
from his ways. Even those entrusted with the
"Ephesian" vision failed and fell away, and indeed the church in Ephesus was foremost in that
failure. If you compare the first Epistle to the
Ephesians with the second Epistle to the
Ephesians—that of Paul with that of Jesus
through John (Rev. 2:1-7)—the two letters show
you where these people are. Something terrible
has happened; and now John is brought in and

commissioned—for what? Not to lead further, but to restore. You will find that, throughout the New Testament, the ministry of John is always restorative. He does not say anything startlingly new and original. He does not introduce anything further, (though it is true that in the Apocalypse he carries what has already been given to its consummation.) What distinguishes John, whether in Gospel, Epistles or Revelation, is his concern to bring the people of God back to a position they have lost.

Once more, this is in keeping with the circumstances of John's call to be a disciple. Peter was called to follow when he was casting a net into the sea; Paul was (presumably) already by trade a tent-maker when God named him a "chosen vessel unto me"; and John was called quite differently again. Like Peter, John was a fisherman, but unlike him he was not in the boat but on the shore of the lake at the moment of his call, and we are told that he and his brother were "mending their nets." When you set yourself to mend something, you seek to bring it back to its original condition. Something has been damaged or lost, and your task is to repair and recover it; and that is the special ministry of John. He is always bringing us back to God's original.

Perhaps that statement may seem to call for fuller explanation, but we will leave that to come in its place. And lest we be thought to make too much of the coincidence of the secular occupations of these three apostles, let it be said at once that we regard these details, providentially recorded as they doubtless are, purely as convenient pegs on which to hang our thoughts, and to help fix in our minds the infinitely greater things for which each of them stood as a servant of God.

So we have before us these three representative men. We have Peter, concerned first with the ingathering of souls; we have Paul, the wise master-builder, building according to the heavenly vision given to him; and then, when failure threatens, we have John introduced to re-affirm that there is an original purpose still in view, and one that, in the mind of God, has never been abandoned. There is still something which he intends to fulfill, and from that intention he will never be deflected.

The practical point of what we have been saying is this, that it takes these three complementary and interrelated ministries to make the Church perfect. It takes the ministry of Peter to initiate things in any given situation; it takes the ministry of Paul to build upon that beginning; and it takes the ministry of John to bring things back, where that has become necessary, into line with God's original intention. Few will deny that the need of each of these three ministries is with us today, or that the third, that of recovery, is perhaps the greatest need of all in this closing period of the age. It will help us therefore to look at some of the key points of each of them in more practical detail, and to give special attention to the present implications of the last of the three.

Accordingly, in the chapters that follow we shall consider in turn Peter, Paul, and John—first the men themselves, and then their characteristic ministries of initiation, construction, and recovery. Let us, as we do so, allow the Spirit of God to speak through them his own personal challenge to each of our hearts.

2
Peter
–and
the Way

One of the features that strike most forcibly any reader of the opening chapters of the book of Acts is the unquestioned authority with which the apostle Peter proclaims the Gospel of salvation through Jesus Christ. He is the first great example of an effective evangelist. Listen to him as he points men to God: "Ye men of Judaea, and all ye that dwell at Jerusalem, ... give ear unto my words.... Repent ye, and be baptized every one of you.... Save yourselves from this crooked generation" (Acts 2:14, 38, 40). "Ye rulers of the

people, and elders, ... be it known unto you all, ...
In none other is there salvation.... We cannot but
speak the things which we saw and heard" (Acts
4:8, 10, 12, 20). In such striking phrases as these
we hear Peter speak as a herald of the Kingdom
proclaiming to men the way of life; and we see
God authenticating his utterances by the manifest presence with him of the Holy Spirit, and by
the deep and lasting work of conviction wrought
in his hearers.

It is important, therefore, that we should understand first of all what it was that qualified
Peter to become God's mouthpiece. For before
Peter could speak he had to be spoken to; before
he could serve as custodian of "the keys of the
kingdom of heaven," he had to encounter the
demands of that Kingdom upon himself.

What is the meaning of the term "kingdom"?
Surely it is the realm of a king. It is the sphere of
his authority, his reign. So when Jesus comes
into his Kingdom, he comes into the place of
power. Wherever the sovereignty of the Lord
Jesus is recognized, there his Kingdom is; and
wherever that sovereignty is not recognized,
there his Kingdom has not yet come. If the Kingdom of God is to be established on earth, then
men must be brought under the unquestioned
rule of God. Man must bow to the absolute authority, dominion and sovereign rule of Jesus
Christ. It is *his Kingdom* that is to come.

It is therefore most helpful to notice what followed in the Gospel narrative upon that promise
to Peter about the keys of the Kingdom. First
there intervened a setback, in which Peter

clearly demonstrated that he was certainly not yet a consistent subject of the Kingdom, but rather a stumbling-block to his Lord. There followed some very striking words, addressed by Jesus to the whole group of his disciples, about the Son of man "coming in his kingdom." And then, only a few days later, these very words found visible expression on the mount of transfiguration, when Peter in particular came in a special way to feel their force.

We know the incident well. Jesus was transfigured before them, presenting to their view in those moments the Kingdom in its nature and essence—though not yet, of course, in its full scope—in the person of the King. Immediately Peter burst out with his spontaneous response. "Not knowing what he said," yet ever ready to say something, he proposed that they should build three tabernacles, one each for Jesus, Moses, and Elijah.

THE FATHER INTERVENES

Three tabernacles—not one! Do you see the import of Peter's brilliant suggestion? There were two very great men there with Jesus in the mount—great not alone for their own sakes but because of what they represented. There was Moses standing for the law, and there was Elijah for the prophets, and, in proposing to prolong the mountaintop experience, Peter would make provision for these two alongside the Lord. They would, of course, be in a subordinate position, but nevertheless they would have some standing beside him and a position of authority to be reckoned with.

But in the *Kingdom* you cannot do that! You cannot have more than one authority. You cannot have a multitude of voices. There can be only one Voice. It was to point this lesson that, "while he yet spake," the Father broke in with what amounted to a rebuke. Interrupting Peter, as though to say: "This is not the time for you to speak but to listen," he directed him to the One who alone has a right to speak in the Kingdom. "This is my beloved Son, ... hear ye him." In other words: "Everything in the Kingdom hangs upon Jesus Christ speaking and upon your paying heed to his words."

We said that Moses and Elijah represent the law and the prophets. God's word makes it clear that now, with the coming of the Kingdom, these were to give way before it. "The law and the prophets were until John: from that time the gospel of the kingdom of God is preached, and every man entereth violently into it" (Luke 16:16). In its very nature the Kingdom supersedes them both. If there is still law, there is no Kingdom; if there are still prophets there is no Kingdom. The law and the prophets must yield to the Kingdom of Jesus Christ; they cannot claim equal place with it. They must not usurp its authority. That is why Peter's speech was brought to a sudden conclusion by the intervention of God. His suggestion was set aside by a definite and deliberate utterance from heaven itself, for the whole basis of the Kingdom was at stake, the very foundation of Christianity was involved. If the Kingdom is to come, then Moses must give place to it, and so must Elijah. If you hold on to the law and the prophets you forfeit the Kingdom, and if you have the Kingdom you must let go the law and the prophets.

Let us think about this a little further, for we want to be quite practical, and at the same time we need to be careful to make no mistake. What is law? And what are the prophets? Well, of course, in the Jewish usage these terms stood together for the whole of the Old Testament Scriptures, and we must be clear first of all that the Lord Jesus never for one moment proposed that these be wholly cast aside. (See, for example: Matthew 5:17, 18; Luke 24:27, 32, 44.) No, I think we must look a little deeper for the principles envisaged here.

The law is the written word which expresses the will of God; the prophets are the living men who also express that will. In Old Testament days God usually expressed his will to ordinary Israelites by one or other of these means. For God dwelt not in man's heart but in an unapproachable Holy of Holies. How then could man inquire of him? First he could do so by reference to the law. Suppose he desired to know the appropriate procedure for dealing with leprosy or defilement with a dead body, or whether or not he might use a particular species of animal or bird for food, he would go with his question to the Book of the law. By careful searching he would find the answer there, and he might do so without direct personal reference to God himself. But suppose instead he wished to know whether or not he should go on a particular journey to a particular place. He might read the Book from beginning to end and nowhere discover even a mention of that place's name. What would he do then? He would turn to a prophet and say, "Kindly enquire of the Lord for me whether I should make this journey or not." But here again the answer came to him second-hand, as it were. He had no authority to go to God direct. Whether through law or prophets, his knowledge of God always came to him indirectly, through a book or through a man, never by direct revelation from God himself.

But that is not Christianity. Christianity always involves a personal knowledge of God through his Spirit, and not merely the knowing of his will through the medium of a man or a book. Many Christians today have a book-knowledge of Christ; they know him indeed through God's own Book, but they have no vital relationship with him. Worse still, many know him only "by hearsay," from their pastor or from some other man, but they are not in direct communication with him. Their knowledge is outward, not inward; and let me affirm that anything short of a personal, inward revelation of the Lord is not Christianity. In seeking to know God's will under the old covenant, men were restricted to the law and the prophets, but under the New Covenant God has promised that "they shall not teach each his fellow-citizen, and each his brother, saying, Know the Lord; because all shall know me in themselves, from the little one unto the great among them" (Heb. 8:11[1]). "You shall know him *in yourselves,*" and knowing him thus it will be unnecessary to refer either to a "brother" or a "neighbor" for information concerning the Lord. Christianity is based not on information but on revelation. That is where the Lord began with Peter in the very passage before us: "Blessed art thou, Simon, ... for flesh and blood hath not revealed it unto thee, but my Father which is in heaven." The Kingdom of God is founded on a personal knowledge of the Lord which comes through a direct speaking by him and a direct hearing by you and me.

Thus, in practical terms today, we have the written Scriptures, represented by Moses, and we have the living human messenger, represented by Elijah who never tasted death. These two God-given gifts to every believer are among the most precious factors that contribute to our Christian life: the Book of God in our hand to instruct us, and the friend who lives close to the Lord and who can often make known to us what the Lord has shown him. The Book is always right; the counsel of a friend so often is. We need God's Book and we need God's prophets. He would not have us discard either. But the lesson of this incident on the mount of transfiguration is surely that neither of these can take the place of the living voice of God to our hearts.

We dare not despise God's messengers. We need again and again the arresting challenge of a

---

[1]J. N. Darby, *New Translation.*

truly prophetic spoken word or the calm of mature spiritual instruction. But we do not commit ourselves totally and exclusively to the revelation which comes through holy men of God, however sound it be. We are under duty bound to listen to the voice of the Lord and to follow him.

Still less dare we despise God's written Word. The inspired Scriptures of truth are vital to our life and progress, and we would not—we dare not—be without them. Nevertheless there are those of us who may be in danger of looking to the letter of the Word even more than to Jesus Christ himself as our final authority. What the Bible says we set ourselves to carry out, religiously and in detail, and God may honor us for that. Yet if, in doing so, we go further, and exalt the Bible to a position where our use of it challenges even the very lordship of Christ himself, we may run the risk of remaining tragically out of touch with *him*.

For the Kingdom is more than these. It involves on the positive side a recognition of the absolute authority of Christ, and on the negative side a repudiation of every authority but his as final. It demands a personal, first-hand intelligence of the will of God, that embraces these other God-given aids but that does not end with them. Christianity is a revealed religion, and revelation is always inward, direct, and personal. That was the lesson Peter had to learn. In the Kingdom there is only one Voice to be heard, through whatever medium it speaks. I still have the written Scriptures and I still have my brother's "prophetic" word (for Moses and Elijah *were* there on the mount!). Christianity is not independent of men and books—far from it. But the way of the Kingdom is that the "beloved Son" speak to me personally and directly, and that personally and directly I *hear him.*

THE SON INTERVENES

We have dealt at some length with what I feel to be a fundamental lesson in the training of Peter as a servant of God. We must now notice two instances in which that lesson is further applied, first to the practical question of personal contact with men, and then to the communication to them of the gospel.

It has always seemed to me that Peter was a man with whom it was easy to talk. It was only too easy to draw him into conversations in which he himself became trapped, as the maid proved later in the courtyard of the high priest's house. Now, only a short time after the events we have discussed, someone approached him with a question about Jesus to which he at once responded with a ready answer (Matt. 17:24). "Doth not your master pay the half shekel?" "Yes," replied Peter, as though to say: "Of course! Naturally he does. Why not?" And having said this, we are told, he went in to Jesus in the house.

Now I want you to notice carefully what it says next. Matthew tells us that "Jesus spake first to him." Peter was apparently on the point of opening his mouth to say something like: "Master,

they have come about the temple tax. We *do* pay
it, don't we?" He was in fact, we might almost
feel, about to tell the Lord what he should do!

But Jesus anticipated Peter with a statement of
his own true position. Is this payment indeed
required of him? No, certainly not! The sons of
the Kingdom are free. There is of course no obligation laid upon them to pay the half shekel. Ah,
but wait a minute! That does not mean that in
this instance it will go unpaid. What Peter has
impetuously committed him to, Jesus will most
certainly pay in full, meeting with a gracious
miracle the situation created by his disciple's
impulsiveness. But let Peter be clear about this
one thing, that Jesus does so, not on the basis of
moral necessity, but of free grace.

Here, then is the new principle with which the
Lord confronts his servant, a principle touching
directly upon the matter of our contact with men
as yet outside the Kingdom. What is it that
should govern our relations with them in order
that they might be won for the Lord? As in this
instance, so always, it is not the will of God as it
may have been revealed to us in its ultimate intention, but rather, that will *as it is expressed
first of all in terms of the Cross of Christ*. God
had never laid it down that his Son must pay the
temple tax, and as Son of God there was no
necessity for him to do anything whatever about
it. Indeed we might feel that for him to do so
would be to put himself in the wrong position of
the "stranger." Then why did he do it? *"Lest we
cause them to stumble."* Has it occurred to you
that the very Son of God himself uttered these

words? There could of course be no question at
any time of his evading a duty; but that was not
the point at issue here. Indeed the situation was
quite different: it was a question rather of his
discarding a privilege. This is the way of the
Cross; and the principle involved is a significant
and searching one.

Think again. Here are two demands upon us
which, superficially at least, may appear to be in
conflict. On the one hand it is perfectly clear
from the Lord's words that the will of God for us
as sons is that we should be free. Let us call this
"God's will A." On the other hand we are presented with a different expression of his will in
the Cross of Christ, and one requiring that, to our
own loss if need be, we forego what we might
enjoy, in order that others be not offended. Call
this "God's will B."[2] How do we reconcile these
two conflicting principles, A and B, exemption
from duty and the sacrifice of privilege?

First, let me make it clear that in this we are
not making provision for the fear of man. The
fear of man is a snare, and we must be delivered
from it. With regard to duty the fear of man has
no place, but only the fear of God. With regard
however to privilege, we may legitimately fear

[2]Put differently, the distinction I am seeking to draw is
between, in the first case, a matter that is between the Lord
and ourselves—will A—and, in the second, a matter between
the Lord, ourselves, *and other people*—will B. The one is
straightforward, between God and me; the other is compli-
cated by the need, *imposed upon me by God*, to consider also
a third party. Such a consideration must have in view *their*
relation, or potential relation, to God, no less than mine.

lest, in asserting our rights, we become guilty of causing men to stumble. There are many things which God shows us personally that come under the head of will A—things that, as children of God, we should expect to be free to do (or to be exempt from doing). If however we try to pursue them, we come up against difficulties with our parents or our family, our employers or perhaps other servants of God, and we are compelled to take into account will B. We have a right to be exempt, but God also tells us something about not giving offense. Which principle are we going to follow?

In his Word God has spoken to us, on the one hand, of "forsaking all and following him," and yet, on the other, of obedience to parents and to husbands, of consideration for wives and children, of subjection to one another in love; and dare we ignore these latter commands? It would almost seem as though God's will comes into conflict with itself here, but that cannot ultimately be the case. We ourselves, of course, if once we have set ourselves to serve God as the Son served the Father, instinctively prefer will A to will B, because the latter brings in a human element which conflicts with our conception of that service, and we do not like it. We would rather hang on to will A—no tribute money—at any cost. Yet what we shrink from is not in fact merely a human element, for, I repeat, it is *God* who has imposed will B. And I want to suggest that, wherever in God's Word provision is made under the heading of will B, the divine principle is that we should do will B *before* will A, doing it in the faith that the Lord himself will eventually bring will A to pass. It is not an abandonment of will A, but a surrendering of it *to him.* Because the Son himself acted thus, so must we.

Often our hearts are so taken up with will A—the liberty and calling of sons—that we feel that we must push through at any cost, and so we find ourselves kicking against everything and everyone in the way, and as a consequence we very soon forfeit our rest and the blessing of God. God's cure for this is, as always, to remind us once again of the action of his Son. The Lord Jesus had absolutely no need to forego the high place that was his *by the will of God*—and yet he "emptied himself." In sheer grace he let go his own preferences, and yielded his soul to the very death of the Cross for our sakes. Recall his words at the great crisis in the garden: "O my Father, if it be possible, let this cup pass away from me; nevertheless, not as I will, but as thou wilt." They reveal what it was that, as Son, he would naturally prefer, but that, as Savior, he would forego. Whatever the cost to himself, *it was impossible for him not to do the will of God.*

For the will of God is never really in conflict with itself. It goes behind "A or B" just as it goes behind "the cup." If we are taken up with "the cup"—with the pros and cons, the effects and contingencies, involved in obeying the Lord—we shall run a grave risk of missing that will. If, on the other hand, we try to push things through in our own way, we get away from the pathway of the Cross. Our attitude should be: God showed me that thing, but I am perfectly prepared to be contradicted, limited, checked if need be, and *to abide God's time*. I must submit myself to his will B, and I have to trust him to bring his will A to pass through it all. It is not necessary for me to force the issue. I can safely entrust it to him. This, I say, is "bearing the cross."

For there are two sides to cross-bearing. The first and obvious one is that the Cross of Christ "crosses out" our own will. We recognize that and assent to it, and thereafter are resolved to serve him and him only. But when that has been settled in principle, we encounter something else. One day it may seem unmistakably clear that it is the will of God for us to do a certain thing, and our heart responds to that and we seize upon it. We have no difficulty, for we truly *want* the will of God. But alas, a little later we find the very thing revealed to be his will is frustrated by events, or, as all too often happens, by others, and with it of course our perfectly sincere and devoted will has to be crossed also—and that is something we do not like at all! This is a second, and often inevitable, effect of bearing the cross.

Let me illustrate. When I was a young man at college in Foochow, God showed me I was to go in my vacation to an island which was infested with pirates, to preach the gospel. It was a step of faith, and it required quite a struggle for me to be willing to do so. I visited the island and found the people willing, and after much difficulty I rented a house, got it repaired and had everything ready. One hundred of the brethren were praying for me, and many had also given money towards the expenses. All this time my parents had said nothing, and then, five days before I was to go and when I was already packed up, they suddenly stepped in and forbade it! The house was ready, the money was spent, the will of God was burning in my heart; what was I to do? My parents, God-fearing folk, said "No"; I was still a student; and God said, "Honor thy father and thy mother." I sought light from God, and God said to me, "Yes, that plan is indeed my will, but it is never my intention that you should bring that will to pass by violence. Wait, and I will work out my will. It is right for you to submit to your parents." I had no liberty to explain to others the reason for my change of plan—that it was my parents who had stopped me—and all, I fear, misunderstood me. It wounded me deeply when the one whose opinion I valued most said, "It will be difficult to trust you in the future."

In God's time the way to that island *was* opened, and his will that souls should be won there came wonderfully to pass. But this experience had taught me an important lesson. I already *liked* that will! Not going was difficult. It cut me; which showed that this particular expression of God's will was in fact now in danger of becoming my will in a possessive way; I had entered into it too much. I had made up my mind to go. If I had had a pure desire for God's will alone to be done, the setback would not have touched me in the way it did. There would have been a detachment of spirit. So God had to allow the disappointment, with its attendant misunderstanding, in order to teach me this valuable lesson.

If a thing is revealed in the Word of God, we dare not cast it aside; we have to submit. If the written Word of God—"honor thy father and thy mother"—cuts across will A, we must wait for him to bring will A to pass. He needs no help to do so. God is seeking to show us that we do not need to push. Self so easily steps in to do the will of God; but God has his time, and he will accomplish it in his own way. Self is fed and nourished because we say, "I am doing God's will." In our eagerness we think nothing on earth should cross that—and then God himself lays something across our path in order to counter this attitude. The most difficult and painful thing for the Cross to do is to cut across our zeal for the will of God and our love for his work. We have to learn that, for the Lord Jesus himself, the Cross was will B—something that, though it cut across his path, was revealed in the Scriptures to be in fact the divinely chosen way to the fulfillment of will A (see Luke 18:31-33). Alone he might have bypassed the Cross, but if others were to have a part with him in the Kingdom, that Cross was necessary. That surely is the meaning of his words in John 17:19: "For their sakes I sanctify myself." The Kingdom and the throne represented will A for him, but the Cross was the way to it. You and I may be 100 percent sure of will A for our lives, but we shall often encounter will B on the road to it. And because of the carnality of our nature, in one way or another the Cross has always to intervene and deal with what is of ourselves, in order that the outcome may be all of God.

In what we have been saying, our eyes have been on the Lord Jesus, not on Peter. Peter himself can have grasped little of this principle, though the day would come when he understood it. One day he would not only see the necessity of the death of the Lord Jesus on his behalf, but would come to be personally identified with that death and ready to face its practical implications in his own experience. "When thou wast young thou girdedst thyself, and walkedst whither thou wouldest: but when thou shalt be old, thou shalt stretch forth thy hands, and another shall gird thee, and carry thee whither thou wouldest not" (John 21:18). To give in *to others* is what we find so hard.

But the Lord Jesus does not press the issue any further with Peter at this time. Instead he performs a gracious miracle, and one which must surely also have been meant to speak as a parable to him. "Go to the sea, and cast a hook, and take up the fish that first cometh up; and when thou hast opened his mouth, thou shalt find a shekel: that take, and give unto them for me and for thee." Yes, *for me and for thee.* Some have remarked that this incident is the only example of the Lord performing a miracle for himself. True, but it was only half for himself, for half was for Peter—and you and I can add, "for me." In that single shekel, meeting by grace the temple tribute for two men, we have wonderfully set forth the intimate union of the servant with his Lord in one Church, one Body.

And the miraculous fish? Does it not assure us that, when we are on a right basis with regard to the will of God, the expenses will be found by God himself? Whenever love has to go further than duty, we can look to the Lord to meet the charges.

THE SPIRIT INTERVENES

But we have not finished with Peter and the interruptions that he suffered so profitably at the hand of God. We have heard the voice of the Father intervene on the mountaintop, and the Son "speak first" in the house. We move on now briefly to Acts chapter 10 and the account of Peter's visit to the house of Cornelius. By now he is in the full stream of his life's ministry as an evangelist. He has witnessed the outpouring of the Spirit at Jerusalem as multitudes were swept into the Kingdom. Overcoming any natural hesitation he might have had, he has been present to witness too the outpouring of the same Spirit upon the Samaritans. Now, quite lately, he has come to Joppa and has been given the strange vision of the "great sheet" coming down from heaven, a vision consistent in some ways with his calling and yet having new and startling implications. "What God hath cleansed, make not thou common." Impelled by these words, he sets out for Caesarea, but it is difficult to avoid the impression of caution, and even of reluctance, that the narrative of his visit creates.

Peter was still a Jew at heart. Even after the vision of the sheet, he went unwillingly and as by compulsion to this Gentile household. He went as a disciplined, if somewhat puzzled, servant of God, but inwardly he seems to have stood, as it were, aloof. He was not yet wholly committed, and could very easily, even now, have stood in God's way.

Then, too, there were those brothers with him—good men from Joppa, but of course lacking the striking personal vision he had thrice received on the housetop. How would they react? And not only they but his own more orthodox fellow apostles and elders in Jerusalem? It would not be surprising if his mind held some real anxiety about their possible reactions, once they came to hear of his visit.

So he opened his mouth and began his sermon. There is nothing lacking in the message he gave. Luke's summary of it reveals a well-constructed setting forth of the essentials of the gospel. What Peter makes clear however is that he never even got half way through! By his own estimate he had· barely "begun to speak" (Acts 11:15) when the Holy Spirit himself intervened and brought him to a full stop.

Notice that Peter had not reached the point of mentioning the Spirit. (Would he have done so had he been allowed to go on?) He got as far as the Cross and remission of sins, and then, while he "yet spake these words, the Holy Spirit fell." The Lord himself assumed command, and Peter had learned enough by now to know that this was the time to stand back. Indeed, there was nothing more to be said. When God acts directly on the audience, the preacher's task is ended.

How gracious it was of God to intervene in this way! Had he waited for Peter to do something—perhaps to baptize or lay hands upon these men (compare Acts 8:17; 19:5, 6)—how would Peter have answered the brethren when he got back to Jerusalem? "This is all your fault, Peter," they would have said. "You started it all. If you had not laid hands on the Gentiles nothing would have happened!" But to the brothers with him at Caesarea Peter had been able to appeal on the ground of God's *fait accompli*, "Can any man forbid the water?" So now to these others in Jerusalem, he can say: "Who was I, that I could withstand God?"

How vividly this illustrates the words of Jesus in Luke: "The gospel of the kingdom is preached, and every man"—Jew, Samaritan and Gentile—"entereth violently into it." The sovereign Lord himself had, as it were, turned the key and opened the door. There can be no questioning the authority of the King. The way to the Kingdom lies open at his command. As Peter had said, but with perhaps greater truth than he as yet knew, "He is Lord of all."

With this principle established in the servant, we can turn in the next chapter to look at the needs of the sinner.

3 Catching Men

How do men press into the Kingdom? We have considered at some length how a preacher of the gospel needs to be personally prepared in spirit for his task. But what of the hearers? What is the minimum requirement in the sinner if he is to find the Lord and be saved? This question now claims our attention, for it is as important for the preacher to know what he is attempting to do as it is for him to be prepared in spirit to do it.

In the discussion which follows we can only deal with a single point in the preaching of the

gospel. I take it for granted that the servant of the
Lord knows the facts of redemption through the
atoning death of Christ, and that he himself is
born of the Spirit. I assume also that he knows
how to present those facts clearly and with
power. I am concerned here not with the sub-
stance of his preaching, but rather with the principles that should guide in the actual task of
leading the individual soul to Christ.

What is necessary for a man to be saved? How
can he be prevailed upon to come to the door of
the Kingdom and enter? How do we bring men
who have only the absolute minimum of knowledge or desire for God into a living touch with
him? These are our questions, and I am going to
lay down four guiding principles that will, I
hope, be found to go a long way towards answer-
ing them.

God has made, from his side, a threefold provision for every man in his hour of crisis. First,
Jesus has come as the Friend of sinners; second,
it is he personally (and no intermediary) whom
men are called to meet; and third, the Holy Spirit
has been poured out upon all flesh, to bring to
pass in man the initial work of conviction of sin,
repentance, and faith, and, of course, all that follows. Then, finally, from the side of the sinner,
one condition and one only is demanded. He is
not required—in *the first place*—to believe, or to
repent, or to be conscious of sin, or even to know
that Christ died. He is required only to approach
the Lord with an honest heart.

This last statement may at first startle you, but
as we go on, I think you will see how helpful it

is. We will, however, take these points in order, beginning from the side of God's provision.

THE SINNER'S FRIEND

In the Gospels the Lord Jesus is presented as the Friend of sinners, for historically he was found, first of all, moving among men as their Friend before he became their Savior. But do you realize that today he is still in the first place our Friend, in order that he may become our Savior? Before we have reached the point where we are willing—or indeed able—to receive him as Savior, he comes to us as a Friend, so that personal encounter is not debarred to us and the door is held open for us to receive him as Savior. This is a precious discovery.

Since I saw the Savior as the Friend of sinners I have seen many unusual and difficult people brought to the Lord. I remember how in one place a young woman came and attacked me, saying that she did not *want* to be saved. She said that she was young and intended to have a good time, and did not want to have to leave her ways and become sedate and sober, for then there would be no joy in life. She said she had no intention of forsaking her sins and had not the least desire for salvation! It transpired that she knew quite a lot about the gospel, for she had been brought up in a mission school, and this was her reaction against it. After she had more or less raved at me for a while, I said, "Shall we pray?" "What should *I* pray?" she replied scornfully. I said, "I can't be responsible for your prayer, but I will pray first, and then you can tell the Lord all that you have been saying to me." "Oh, I couldn't do that!" she said, somewhat taken aback. "Yes, you can," I replied. "Don't you know that he is the Friend of sinners?" This touched her. She did pray—a very unorthodox prayer—but from that hour the Lord worked in her heart, for in a couple of days' time she was saved.

It is clear from the New Testament that the Lord Jesus came as a Friend, *in order to help sinners to come to him.* Our coming to him was made possible by his first coming to us. He came to bring heaven down within our reach. I remember that I was once sitting talking to a brother in his home. His wife and mother were upstairs, but his small son was in the sitting-room with us. Presently the little fellow wanted something, and called out to his mother for it. "It is up here," she replied; "come up and get it." But he cried out to her, "I can't, Mummy, it's such a long way. *Please* bring it down to me." And indeed he was very small; so she brought it down. And salvation is just like that. Only by his coming right down to us could our need be met. Had he not come, sinners could not have approached him; but he came down in order to lift them up.

At the hour of crisis there are many practical difficulties that face the sinner. For example, in the Scriptures we are often told to believe. The Word lays much stress on the necessity of faith. But you say, "I have not got faith." A girl once said to me, "I can't believe. I would like to believe but I can't! My parents keep on saying to me 'You *must* believe,' but it is no good; I haven't got it in me. The desire is there, but I find faith lacking. It is *impossible* to believe." "That is all right," I said. "You can't believe. But you can ask the Lord to give you faith. He is prepared to help you to that extent. You pray: 'Lord, help thou my unbelief.' "

Or again, the Word tells us that we are to repent. What if we have no desire whatever to repent? I met a student once who said it was too early for him to come to the Lord. He wanted more time in which to taste the pleasures of sin and to enjoy himself. He said to me, "The thief on the cross was saved, but he had had his fling, and it was high time that he repented. But I—I am young." "Well, what do you want to do?" I asked him. He replied, "I want to wait for another forty years and have a good time, and then I will repent." So I said, "Let us pray." "Oh, I can't pray," he answered. "Yes, you can," I said. "You can tell the Lord all you have told me. He is the Friend of unrepentant sinners like you." "Oh, I couldn't say *that* to him." "Why not?" "Oh, but I could not." "Well, be quite honest. Whatever is in your heart, you tell it to him. He will help you." Finally he prayed, and told the Lord that he did not want to repent and be saved, but that he knew he needed a Savior; and he just cried to him for help. The Lord worked repentance in him and he got up a saved man.

In England in the early 19th century there was a woman who had Christian parents and who for years had longed to be saved. She went to hear this and that preacher and visited churches and chapels in her search for salvation, but all in vain. One day she wandered into a little chapel with no real expectation in her heart, for she was almost in despair. She sat down at the back. The speaker was an elderly man. Suddenly in the middle of his address he stopped and pointing his finger at her said: "You, Miss, sitting there at the back, you can be saved *now*. You don't need to *do* anything!" Light flashed into her heart, and with it, peace and joy. Charlotte Elliott went home and wrote her well-known hymn: "Just as I am, without one plea ... O Lamb of God I come." Those words have pointed to countless sinners the way of humble access to God through the blood of Christ. Yes, we dare to say today, to every one of the inhabitants of Shanghai or of any other city, that they can come to him and be saved *just as they are*.

I repeat these incidents just to emphasize that what the sinner cannot do the Savior is at hand to do for him. It is for this reason that we can tell people that they need not wait for anything, but can come to him immediately. Whatever their state, whatever their problem, let them bring it and tell it to the Friend of sinners.

FIRST CONTACT WITH THE LORD

What is salvation? Many think that to be saved we must first believe that the Lord Jesus died for us, but it is a strange fact that nowhere in the New Testament does it say precisely that. Of course the whole message of the New Testament is that Jesus died and rose again that we might be saved. But read through your New Testament carefully and tell me where you can find one verse that says that the condition for being saved is to *believe* that Christ died for our sins. You cannot find it anywhere. We are told to believe *in* Jesus, or to believe *on* him; not to believe *that he died* for us. "Believe on the Lord Jesus Christ and thou shalt be saved" were Paul's words. We are to believe first of all in *him;* not specifically in what he has done.

In John 3:16 we are told that "whosoever believeth on him" shall have everlasting life. Earlier in his Gospel John says that "he came unto his own, and they that were his own received him not." At the end of the same Gospel John states that he wrote it "that ye may believe that Jesus is the Christ, the Son of God; and that believing ye may have life in his name." Men rejected him, not on the ground of what he did but of who he was, and they are invited to believe in what he is and who he is, and not, first of all, in what he has done. John 3:16 does not say: "Whosoever believeth that Christ died for him and bore his sins on the Cross hath everlasting life." Its message is that God gave his Son, and it is he himself in person upon whom we are to believe. "He that hath the Son hath the life."

Of course I do not want you to think me a modernist, who would dare to belittle the Cross or give a lower place to the substitutionary work of Christ. I *do* believe in the necessity of his atonement, and so, I am sure, do you. I trust you will not misunderstand me therefore when I say that the appreciation of that work may not be the *first* step in the sinner's initial contact with the Lord. That appreciation must follow, but the main question is whether or not we have the Son, and not, first of all, whether or not we understand the whole plan of salvation. The first condition of salvation is not knowledge, but meeting *Christ*.

There are many people of whom you may feel that they were saved by the wrong scriptures! They were spoken to through verses that do not seem to point the way of salvation, and you almost feel they cannot be saved on that basis! You feel that there must be a weakness somewhere, and yet you have to recognize that God is often pleased to work in that way. I used to wish that those whom I led to the Lord would be saved on the basis of John 3:16 or 5:24 or 6:40. But I have come to see that all that is needed for the *initial* step is that there should be a personal touch with God, and when that is so the rest will surely follow. It does not matter, therefore, which verses God elects to use for that first step. After all, we do not need to study the theory of electricity and to understand it thoroughly before we can turn on the electric light. The light does not say, "I am not going to shine for you, for you know nothing of the principle on which I work." And God does not set understanding as the condition of our approach to him. "This is life eternal, that they should know thee, the only true God, and Jesus Christ whom thou hast sent."

Let us take three examples from the Gospels. Which was the first outstanding conversion recorded in the New Testament? Surely that of the thief on the cross. Up till then everything had been pointing forward to the Cross of Christ. Now it was being enacted before men's eyes, and the thief was a witness. This man was a model sinner and was receiving a model punishment, and his was, we may say, a model conversion. Yet did he recognize the Lord as Savior? What were his words? "Remember me when thou comest in thy kingdom" (Luke 23:42). What did the Lord reply? He did not remind him of his evil life, or tell him that he was suffering justly and *ought* to die, and that instead he, Jesus, was suffering on the cross for him and dying for his sins. It seems to us that it would have been an excellent opportunity to announce the plan of redemption—but no, the Lord only answered: "Today shalt thou be with me in paradise." For the thief *recognized who Jesus was*—that though suffering unjustly he was going to reign and would have a Kingdom—and he believed *in the Lord*, and that was enough.

Consider next the woman with an issue. In Mark 5:24 we are told that the multitude "thronged" Jesus. There were many among the crowd who were touching and even pressing upon him, but only one among them was healed. She was healed because with a special intention she "touched" him. And it only required a touch; for in her it represented a reaching out in spirit to God for help in her deep need.

Or recall the incident of the Pharisee and the publican at prayer in the temple. The Pharisee understood all about offerings and sacrifices and tithes, but there was from him no cry of the heart to God. But the publican cried, "Lord, have mercy upon me!" Something went out from him to God which met with an immediate response, and the Lord Jesus singles him out as the one whom God reckoned righteous. For what is it to be reckoned righteous? It is *to touch God*.

The Epistle to the Romans tells us in much detail about sin and about the way of salvation, and from a study of it we can learn a great deal about the doctrine of redemption; and yet it was written for the saved. John's Gospel, on the other hand, gives no doctrine in any systematic form; in fact, there seems to be little or no plan to the book at all; and yet it was written for the world (John 20:31). We would have arranged things the other way round, I am sure; and we should have been wrong! For consider: if your house is on fire and there is no way of escape for those on the top story, and if the firemen come and set up a ladder to save you, what will you do? Will you say, "Not so fast! Tell me first why your ladder sticks up without any support. Ordinary ladders have to lean against something. And what material are your clothes made of? Why do they not catch fire?"—and so on? No, you will allow yourself to be saved, and afterwards you may inquire all about the fire escape and the firemen's uniforms and everything else that interests you.

After I was saved I used to feel very dissatisfied with Peter's sermon on the day of Pentecost. Indeed I thought it was, in some respects, a very poor one, for it seemed so inadequate for its purpose. It did not, I thought, make things clear at all, for there is nothing in it about the plan of redemption. What does Peter say? "Jesus of Nazareth, a man approved of God unto you by mighty works and wonders and signs, which God did by him in the midst of you, even as ye yourselves know; him, being delivered up by the determinate counsel and foreknowledge of God, ye by the hand of lawless men did crucify and slay: whom God raised up...." Surely, I felt, here was the golden opportunity Peter needed to press the point home. Surely here was the time to introduce some reference to Isaiah 53, or otherwise to explain the doctrine of the atonement. But no, he let the opportunity pass, and went on: "Let all the house of Israel therefore know assuredly, that God hath made him both Lord and Christ, this Jesus whom ye crucified." How strange that Peter did not even use the title "Savior"! But nevertheless, what was the result? The people, we are told, were pricked in their heart, and cried, "What shall we do?"

Later on Peter went to Gentiles who had a different religious background altogether. There surely, you feel, the gospel would be plainly preached. Yet to Cornelius Peter only spoke about who Christ was, and though he certainly mentioned the remission of sins he gave no explanation of the meaning of his death—yet even so, the Holy Spirit fell upon them all.

Surely it becomes clear from this that salvation is not initially a question of knowledge but of "touch." All who touch the Lord receive life. We might say that, judged by his sermons in the Acts, even Paul was not clear in his gospel.

Those many years ago the gospel was not preached as it is now! There was not the same clear presentation of truth! But *is* it the truth which is the most important? The great weakness of the present preaching of the gospel is that we try to make people *understand* the plan of salvation, or we try to drive people to the Lord through the fear of sin and its consequences. Wherein have we failed? I am sure it is in this, that our hearers do not see *him*, for we do not adequately present the Person. They only see "sin" or "salvation," whereas their need is to see the Lord Jesus himself, and to meet him and "touch" him.

Too often those who have been saved merely through knowledge develop big heads. They progress without seeming to feel much need of God. They *know* it all and they even feel qualified to criticize the preacher's presentation of facts. But when it comes to a crisis in which they lose their known bearings and have to trust the Lord over something, they cannot do so. They are not in living touch with him. Yet there are others, who may know very little but have come out of themselves, and have touched the living God, who develop and grow in faith even through the severest trial. That is why our first object must be to lead people to meet him.

None of us can fathom the mysterious ways of God. None of us dare prescribe for him how he should work. There was a Chinese boy who, when he was twelve years old, was taken by his mother up to a temple in the hills. As he was worshiping before the shrine with his mother, he looked at the idol and thought, "You are too ugly and too dirty to be worshiped. I don't believe you can save me. What is the sense of worshiping you?" But out of respect for his mother he joined in the ceremony, and after it was over his mother got into her chair to go down the mountain. But he slipped away to the back of the temple and found an open space where he stood and looked up to heaven and said, "O God, whoever you are, I do not believe that you can dwell in that shrine. You are too big, and it is too small and dirty for you. You surely must dwell right up there in the heavens. I do not know how to find you, but I put myself in your hands; for sin is very strong, and the world pulls. I commit myself to you, wherever you may be." Thirty years later I met him and told him the gospel. He said, "I have met the Lord Jesus for the first time today, but this is the second time that I have touched God. Something happened to me that day thirty years ago on the mountaintop."

It is the living Lord who becomes our Savior. Jesus is no longer the crucified but the reigning One, and today therefore we go for salvation not to the foot of the Cross but to the Throne, to believe in him as Lord. Perhaps we need to see more clearly the difference between redemption and salvation. Redemption was secured by the Lord Jesus on the Cross two thousand years ago. Our salvation rests today upon that redemption, accomplished once for all in time. Nevertheless it is equally true that you may have been "saved" ten, twenty, or thirty years ago and I quite recently, because for each of us salvation is a personal matter—a personal partaking, as it were, of Christ. There is surely a parallel here with the Israelites of old in Egypt. The redeemed firstborn was to partake of the Passover sacrifice *by eating the meal,* and not merely to observe the shed blood of his redemption upon the door posts, where God had caused it to be placed for his own purposes of atonement.

It comes to this, that salvation, which is a personal and a subjective experience, may be said to rest rather upon the Lord's resurrection than upon his death. The death of Christ was necessary for atonement objectively before God. But for salvation the New Testament lays emphasis upon our faith in his resurrection, for the resurrection is the proof that his death has been accepted. We believe *in the Lord Jesus Christ,* personally risen and ascended to glory, and we seek to bring sinners *now* into immediate contact with him.

AN HONEST HEART TOWARDS GOD

Before we come to the third provision that God has made for the crisis of salvation in a man's life, I am going to digress, and to deal first with what seems to me to be the single requirement demanded from man himself.

When you have preached the gospel of repentance and of faith through Jesus Christ for the remission of sins, you encounter various difficulties in your hearers which may bring you up short. One man, having heard you tell all about sin and its punishment, says quite frankly, "Yes,

I know it all, but I *like* sinning." What will you do? As we have suggested, the Friend of sinners is the One to help him here. Another man listens to you and assents to everything, and yet does not seem to be able to take it in. You meet him next day, and he says, "I have forgotten the third point. What was it?" Salvation is not a question of "points"! Salvation is not even a question of understanding or of will. It is, as we have seen, a question of meeting God—of men coming into firsthand contact with Christ the Savior. So what, you ask me, is the minimum requirement in a man to make that contact possible?

For my reply I would turn you to the parable of the sower. It seems to me that here we are plainly told the one thing that God does demand. "That in the good ground, these are such as in an honest and good heart, having heard the word, hold it fast, and bring forth fruit with patience" (Luke 8:15). What God demands of man is "an honest and good heart"—good, because honest. It does not matter if a man wants or does not want to be saved, it does not matter if he understands or does not understand; provided that he is prepared to be honest with God about it, God is prepared to meet him.

The question has been raised: How do you reconcile God's requirements of "an honest and good heart" with the statement that "the heart is deceitful above all things" (Jer. 17:9)? But the point in the parable of the sower is not that the man who receives the Word is a perfectly honest man in God's eyes, but that he is honest *towards* God. Whatever is in his heart, he is prepared to come to God frankly and openly with it. Of course, it is a fact, and it remains a fact, that the heart of man is "deceitful above all things," but it is still possible for a man with a deceitful nature to turn honestly to God. A dishonest man can come to God and say honestly to him, "I am a sinner; have mercy on me!" In the realm of desire towards God he can be true. This is what God seeks in men, and something of this meaning is contained in the word which says: "The eyes of the Lord run to and fro throughout the whole earth, to show himself strong in the behalf of them whose heart is perfect toward him" (2 Chron. 16:9).

The basic condition of a sinner's salvation is not belief or repentance, but just the honesty of heart towards God. God requires nothing of him but that he come in that attitude. Into that spot of straightforwardness that lies in the midst of much deceitfulness, the good seed falls and brings forth fruit. Of the two thoroughly dishonest thieves crucified with the Lord, there was in the one a little bit of honest desire. The publican who prayed in the temple was a crooked man, but in him too there was that honesty to acknowledge his sinfulness and cry to God for mercy. And what of Saul of Tarsus? He certainly lacked even the desire for salvation through Jesus Christ, but the Lord saw in him on the Damascus road an honest heart Godward, and that was the starting-point of his history with the Lord. He honestly touched the Lord when he said, "Lord, what wilt thou have me to do?" and that "touch" was enough to save him instantly.

For it is the *fact* of the gospel, making possible the initial touch with Jesus Christ, that saves the sinner, and not the sinner's understanding of it.

As several of the incidents recounted earlier have indicated, we should encourage every sinner to kneel down with an honest heart and pray, telling the Lord frankly where he stands. As Christians we are told that we must pray in the name of the Lord Jesus (John 14:14; 15:16; 16: 23, 24), by which, of course, we understand not a mere formula of words but an act of faith in him. But with sinners it is different, for there are prayers which God will hear that are not uttered in the name of Jesus. In Acts 10:4 the angel says to Cornelius: "Thy prayers and thine alms are gone up for a memorial before God." If there is a sincere cry from the heart, God hears. A sinner's heart can touch God.

A striking example of one who came to God without even wanting to be saved is afforded by the experience of an English lady of the last century. One of a wealthy family of good social position, she was well educated, a good musician and an accomplished dancer, and she was both young and beautiful. One night there was a ball to which she was invited. She had a wonderful ball dress specially made for the occasion, and that night she was the one who compelled most attention and was most sought after by all. It was, one might say, a great triumph for her.

After the ball was over she went home, took off her ball dress and cast it aside. She flung herself down and said, "O God, I have everything I want, wealth, popularity, beauty, youth—and yet I am absolutely miserable and unsatisfied. Christians would tell me that this is a proof that the world is empty and hollow, and that Jesus could save me and give me peace and joy and satisfaction. But I don't want the satisfaction that he could give. I don't want to be saved. I hate you and I hate your peace and joy. But, O God, give me what I don't want, and if you can, make me happy!" It is recorded that she got up from her knees a saved woman, and became one who knew the Lord in a deep way.

I affirm once again: all that is needed is an honest heart. If you *want* God there is no difficulty. But praise God, even if you do *not* want him, he will still hear you if you will come to him and be honest about it.

THE HELPER NEAR AT HAND

We have said that a cry to God from the heart is sufficient. In the words of Joel, quoted by Peter: "Whosoever shall call on the name of the Lord shall be saved." How is this possible? Because God has fulfilled the other promise (quoted by Peter from the same prophecy) that: "I will pour forth of my Spirit upon all flesh" (Acts 2:17, 21). Because the Holy Spirit has been poured out upon all mankind, a cry is enough.

No preacher of the gospel is of much use unless he believes this. The presence of the Holy Spirit, and his proximity to the sinner, is vital to our preaching. God in the heavens is too far away; he is, as it were, out of reach of man. But to the Romans Paul writes: "Say not in thy heart, who shall ascend into heaven? (that is, to bring Christ down:) ... The word is nigh thee.... For whosoever shall call upon the name of the Lord shall be saved" (Rom. 10:6, 8, 13).

I always believe that the Holy Spirit is upon a man when I preach to him. I do not mean to say that the Spirit is *within* the hearts of unbelievers, but that he is outside. What is he doing? He is waiting, waiting to bring Christ into their hearts. The Holy Spirit is waiting to enter the heart of the hearer of the gospel. He is like the light. Open the window-shutters even a little and it will flood in and illumine the interior. Let there be but a cry from the heart to God, and *at that moment* the Spirit will enter and begin his transforming work of conviction and repentance and faith—the miracle of new birth.

Not only had Peter observed the miraculous intervention of the Holy Spirit upon his hearers as he preached to them in the home of Cornelius; he had also, of course, his personal experience of the Spirit's work in his own heart. "As I began to speak," he reports, "the Holy Ghost fell on them, *even as on us at the beginning*" (Acts 11:15). Perhaps the biggest condition of success in bringing men to Christ is to remember that the same Holy Spirit, who came to our help in the hour of darkness, is at hand waiting to enter and illumine their hearts also, and to make good the work of salvation to which, in crying to God, they have opened the door.

I had a friend who was preaching in a certain city. A woman sought him out and he talked to her and preached Christ to her. He spoke of her sin, and of the punishment for sin, and of the Lord who came to save. But the woman said to him, "I don't think you know how nice sin is; you have never tasted its delights. I *like* to sin. Life would be empty otherwise." After a while my friend suggested that they pray. The woman said, "What could one so sinful as I say to your God? I cannot find repentance in my heart. I have nothing I could say that would be acceptable to him." But my friend replied: "My God understands. He is *near* to you and he can hear *any* prayer; so you say to him just what you have said to me." She was amazed, for till now she had only heard the kind of formal prayer where you have to say what you do not believe, for politeness's sake! Then he showed her the verse in Acts 11 where it says of the Gentiles on whom the Holy Ghost fell that God "granted" them repentance unto life. So she prayed, and told it all to the God who understands sinners. "Though I do not want to repent," she pleaded. "O God, help me and grant me repentance." And he did! She had opened to his Spirit's illumination the windows of her heart, and she arose from her knees a saved woman.

Here then is a principle, that because Jesus is the Friend of sinners, and because the Holy Spirit undertakes to do what men themselves cannot do, therefore sinners can come to God just as they are. *They do not need to change at all*, and it is not necessary for them to find *in themselves* the ability to do anything. If a man asks you to tell him the gospel of salvation and afterwards he says to you, "Sir, I want to be saved," and on your telling him to believe, he replies, "I can't believe," what will you do? Will you say, "I am afraid you are no good. You go away, and come back when you *can* believe"? Are you not thereby asking him to do something towards his salvation? Another man says to you, "I don't *want* to be saved." What will you do then? Will you send him off to wait until some difficulty or sorrow drives him to God? May you not thereby be closing the door to him? Why need we lay down so many conditions for sinners before they can be saved? Surely if Jesus is the Friend of sinners all men can come as they are, and because his Spirit is at hand to work, we can count on him to do in them what they themselves can never do.

During the twenty years that I have preached the gospel in China, many of course *have* initially understood the way of salvation, many *have* first of all been convicted of sin, *have* repented, *have* believed—and they have come to Christ on that basis and been saved. But, praise God, there have also been many others who, though they did not in the first place repent or believe, or even consciously desire to be saved, yet were persuaded to come honestly to the Lord and make personal contact with him; and in many of these, too, understanding, conviction, repentance, and faith have followed, and they have, as a result, been gloriously saved. This gives me the confidence to state unequivocally that *there is not one other condition necessary to being saved except that of being a sinner and being honest enough to say so to the Lord*. That condition is enough to allow the Holy Spirit to begin his convicting and transforming work.

We have spoken of those who won't repent, and of those who cannot believe; we have spoken of those who have no desire for salvation, and of those who think they are too bad to be saved; we have spoken of those who are confused and cannot understand the gospel, and of those who understand but will not acknowledge the claim of God upon them. May I tell you that it is yet possible for any of these to be saved? I have met all of these six types of people and many of them have been saved on the spot; and in addition I have met a seventh type—those who do not believe there is a God at all—and I have dared to say even to them that they do not need first to substitute theism for atheism. They can be saved *as they are*, even without any belief in God at all, if they will be honest about it.

Some will at once rejoin: "But what about Hebrews 11:6? Surely that verse demands faith in God's existence at least." Well, there was a time when I should certainly have said so, but one day I learned afresh how infinitely far God is prepared to go to meet the son returning from the far country. It happened in the following way.

I was once holding evangelistic meetings in a college in South China. There I met an old friend, in fact, an old schoolfellow. He had been in America and was now in this college as professor of psychology. He had made up his mind about religion and had been in the habit of telling his students that he could explain all so-called conversions on purely psychological grounds. Before the meetings began I went to call on him, and preached to him Christ. Out of politeness he had to listen for a while, but finally he smiled and said, "It is no good preaching to me. I don't believe there *is* a God." I said, perhaps a little rashly, "Even if you do not believe in a God, just pray. You will discover something." He laughed. "Pray, when I don't even believe in a God!" he exclaimed; "how could I?" Then I said, "Though you cannot find a ladder up to God it does not alter the fact that he has come down to find you. You pray!" He laughed again; but I still urged him to do so. I said, "I have a prayer that even you can pray. Say this: 'O God, if there is no God, then my prayer is useless and I have prayed in vain; but if there is a God, then somehow make me know it.' " He replied, "But what has this hypothetical God got to do with Jesus Christ? Where does Christianity come in?" I told him just to add a sentence to his prayer asking God to show him this also. I explained that I was not asking him to admit there was a God; I was not asking him to admit anything; but that there was one thing and one thing only that I asked of him, and that was that he must be honest. His heart must be in his prayer. It must not just be an empty repeating of words. I was not sure that I had accomplished anything; but when I went away I left with him a Bible.

The next day, at the end of the first meeting of my campaign, I asked any who had been saved to stand up, and the first one to do so was this professor. I went up to him afterwards and asked him, "Has anything happened?" He replied,

"Much. I am saved." "How did it happen?" I asked. He replied, "After you went I picked up the Bible and opened it at John's Gospel. My eye caught the words: 'The day after,' 'the next day,' 'the day after,' and I thought to myself, this man knows what he is talking about. He *saw* it all. It is like a diary. After that, I thought about what you had said to me, and I tried to see if there was any catch in it—if you were getting at me in any way. I went over it point by point and could see no flaw in it. It all seemed perfectly sound. Why should I not pray as you suggested? But suddenly the thought came to me: What if there *is* in fact a God? Where do I stand then? Having told my students that there is nothing in religion at all, and that psychology accounts for everything, am I willing to admit to them that I have been wrong all the time? I weighed this up carefully, but nevertheless I felt I had to be honest about it. For if, after all, there really was a God, I would be a fool not to believe in him!

"So I knelt down and prayed; and as I prayed I just *knew* there was a God. How I knew, I cannot explain, but I just knew it! Then I remembered the Gospel of John that I had read, and how it seemed to be written by an eyewitness, and I knew that if that was so, then Jesus was the Son of God—and I was saved!"

Oh, it is wonderful what our God can do! When you go out preaching the gospel, never lose sight of the fact that he is *a living God*, ready to act in mercy. Even if men could be a little better than they are it would not help matters, and if they were much worse it would not hinder. All he looks for is "an honest and good heart." And never forget that the Holy Spirit is present in power to move men's hearts to God. Have faith in him in respect of every soul with whom you have to deal. Alone you may not be much of a fisherman, but cooperating with the Spirit of God, you may have confidence enough to land the biggest fish.

4
Paul and the Life

As we move on now to consider the special contribution in the New Testament of the ministry of the apostle Paul, we shall once again be compelled to take a great deal for granted. For I must repeat that it will be his "specific" ministry that we shall have in mind here, namely, that represented in our analogy by the figure of a "tent." But in dealing thus especially with the collective or corporate theme in his ministry we do not overlook the very wide range of spiritual revelation given to Paul on other matters, such as the divine plan of redemption and the individual believer's growth in Christ.

The letter to the Romans was written, as we have seen, not to show sinners how to enter the door of the Kingdom, but to show us as Christians how God made it possible for us to do so, and what are the consequences of our entry. With this as his object, Paul enlarges in that letter on the great themes of justification and sanctification, of deliverance from sin and from the law, of eternal life in Christ and the walk in the Spirit, and of sonship and the purpose of God. We have dealt at length with some of these matters elsewhere,[1] and have shown that the key to faith and experience in relation to all these things is the opening of our eyes to the great historic fact of Jesus Christ, crucified, risen, and exalted, and with it, to the further fact of our death, resurrection and exaltation with him. God has judged our sins and passed upon our fallen nature the sentence of death, and that sentence has been carried out upon us in Christ. We are received into his Kingdom on the basis, not of our somehow escaping judgment, but of our *having been* judged in him, and our *having been* raised in him to newness of life. The Cross of Christ is for us the gateway to everything.

With this principle established, Paul next sets before us, in a remarkably vivid chapter (Romans 7), first of all his total failure *as a believer* to live the Christian life in his own natural strength, and then his glorious discovery (expanded in

Chapter 8) that nevertheless this *is* possible "through Jesus Christ our Lord." The power of Christ indwelling—"the law of the Spirit of life in Christ Jesus"—is superior to the law of sin and death in his members. In the words of Philippians 4:13, "I can do all things in him that strengtheneth me."

Thus for Paul, the Christian life was a continual miracle—a paradox in which the divine life planted within by new birth shone forth through the "mortal body" of one who consciously walked after the Spirit. "If Christ is in you, the body is dead because of sin; but the spirit is life because of righteousness" (Rom. 8:10). Before we proceed to consider Paul as "tentmaker," and his understanding of the House of God (to which the Epistle to the Romans itself inevitably leads), we will pause to look at the man himself, and to learn a lesson from this personal paradox, so strikingly exemplified in him, of the "earthly house of our tabernacle" and the "earnest of the Spirit" enshrined within it (2 Cor. 5:1-5).

In considering the apostle Paul, I wish to direct your attention to his Second Epistle to the Corinthians, and to ask you first of all to note its special character. The peculiarity of this letter lies in its expression of Paul's inner life and experience. It is the most personal of his letters—indeed of all the New Testament epistles—and without it we should know far less than we do of the man himself. Paul did not want to write the letter, but because of the attitude of the Corinthians God permitted it to be written, and in doing so he allows us to see something which the other Epistles partly conceal. They are full of teaching; this lifts the curtain briefly on the man behind the teaching. *They* present the revelation of God to us; this letter shows us the kind of man to whom God entrusts that revelation.

A few minutes' thought will, I think, suffice to confirm this. In 1 Corinthians 1 Paul writes of God's choice of "the weak things"; 2 Corinthians shows us the grim reality, in Paul himself, of a divinely imposed weakness. In 1 Corinthians 3 Paul is appealing for unity; 2 Corinthians 1 reveals that, for all their rebuffs, he who so strongly exhorted them against factions still counted himself one of them. Further on in 1 Corinthians, after some exceedingly firm dealing with the irregularities at Corinth, Paul follows in chapter 13 with his classic treatment of love; but in 2 Corinthians 2 he explains, concerning the apparent harshness of that earlier letter, how "out of much affliction and anguish of heart I wrote unto you with many tears; not that ye should be made sorry, but that ye might know the love which I have more abundantly unto you." Later still, in 1 Corinthians 16, Paul has to exhort his readers to a practical care for the needs of others; while 2 Corinthians 11 lets us into the secret of how he himself acted in money matters. For it is a principle that there never was a man not clear in respect of money who could really serve God; he who is wrong there is wrong everywhere. Finally, and most relevant to our present purpose, 1 Corinthians 15 gives us the clearest teaching in the New Testament on the subject of the resurrection; but already 2 Corinthians 1 finds Paul himself despairing even of life, "that we should not trust in ourselves, but in God which raiseth the dead."

For Paul, doctrine is everywhere backed by experience. Nothing else constitutes any basis for ministry, whatever men may think about it today. A ministry that is built upon mere theory leads only to impoverishment; a ministry of life springs essentially from experience. 1 Corinthians is concerned with gifts and preaching, 2 Corinthians with life. Because the death of Christ works in him, Paul has life; and because he has life, others have life. The ministry of 1 Corinthians, and indeed of all his Epistles, is based on the man of 2 Corinthians.

THE TREASURE IN THE EARTHEN VESSEL

Now let us go further, and turn our attention to something that arises out of all this, namely the element, already alluded to, of seeming contradiction in Paul.

As we read 2 Corinthians carefully we seem to meet two persons: Paul in himself, and Paul in Christ. Those who observed him found him an anomaly. Lowly and weak in bodily presence, unskilled and of no account in speech, yet somehow he was confident and of good courage, rich in knowledge and strong and weighty in his letters (see 10:1, 10; 11:6), and his dealings with men were always marked by consistency, a fact made possible by his steadfast resolve to know them no longer "after the flesh" but always only in Christ (1:17; 5:16). Inwardly, too, there was the same seeming contradiction in his make-up, as becomes abundantly clear in several passages where he uses the significant words, "but," "yet," "nevertheless." "We despaired," he writes; "we that are in this tabernacle do groan; we were afflicted; without were fightings, within were fears; *nevertheless* God comforted us—God who raiseth the dead." (See 1:8, 9; 5:4; 7:5, 6.)

And not only was this dual consciousness a present experience with him at the time he wrote 2 Corinthians, but there are two great passages which show that it was a usual experience. (See 4:8-10; 6:8-10). Indeed almost everything Paul speaks of, from the opening chapter of the Epistle to its conclusion, is in this one strain. There is one governing principle throughout, which we may best summarize in his own words: "We have this treasure in earthen vessels, that the exceeding greatness of the power may be of God, and not from ourselves" (4:7). In the very first chapter we see "this treasure" in an earthen vessel, and right to the last chapter we keep meeting the earthen vessel—but we keep meeting the treasure also.

"We have this treasure in earthen vessels." This is possibly the clearest statement there is of the nature of practical Christianity. Christianity is not the earthen vessel, nor is it the treasure, but it is *the treasure in the earthen vessel*.

All people, whether Christians or not, have their ideal man. All have their own particular conceptions of what constitutes a good man. They think that if a man does such-and-such things, or behaves in some particular way, or if he is a certain kind of person, that man is good. We have each a set standard in our minds, and if a man measures up to that we call him a "good" man. Before we were saved we had a certain standard, but of course after our salvation we came to see that many whom we admired before were not really to be admired. We judge them now by our newfound light, and we see that they come short. Our scale of measurement has altered.

We even had our ideas about Christ. Before we were saved we had certain opinions about him, but after our salvation those opinions were all thrown out of gear as the Holy Spirit opened our eyes to something of his true nature. As a result, we now have a new standard of Christian living, and we make that on the one hand the goal towards which we ourselves strive and on the other hand the measure by which we judge others. So far so good; but when all this has been said, I want to suggest to you that God's thoughts as to what constitutes a true Christian may even yet take more into account than ours do, and that as a consequence he may require us still further to adjust our thinking regarding ourselves and others.

What is our conception of holiness? Too readily we think of it as the absence of the earthen vessel. We imagine that if we can reach a stage where we have, ourselves, so controlled our affections and emotions that there is virtually no more trace of them, then we have attained to holiness. We fancy that to suppress our feelings, so as to be insensible to suffering or untouched by natural relationships, is a proof of spirituality. In effect, we think that to become spiritual is to cease to be human, and many of us are engaged in covering over the earthen vessel in the mistaken idea that, if it can no longer be seen, that is holiness.

You can tell at once when someone is doing this because he is so unnatural. He dare not let himself go. He dare not speak or act freely, lest the earthen vessel be disclosed. But such a man does not know what true Christianity is. He is artificial, and he uses his artificiality to conceal his actual condition. He schools himself so that the earthen vessel shall not appear. And alas, many think that if only they can get to the state where they do not care what is done or said in their presence, they have indeed attained to Christian holiness.

When I first became a Christian, I too had my own conception of what a Christian was, and I tried my utmost to be that kind of Christian. I thought that if only I could attain to the standard I had conceived, I should have achieved my object. To be a true Christian was my sincere ambition, but of course I had my own mentality as to what that meant. I thought a true Christian should smile from morning to night! If at any time he shed a tear, he had ceased to be victorious. I thought, too, that a true Christian must be an unfailingly courageous person. If under any circumstances he showed the slightest sign of fear, I reasoned that he failed seriously, in that he lacked the faith to trust the Lord. He had in fact fallen short of my standard.

I retained these clearly defined ideas as to what a Christian should be until, one day, I read 2 Corinthians and came to the passage where Paul said he was sad. "As sorrowful...." I read (6:10), and I was arrested. "Paul sorrowful!" I thought. Then I read that he shed "many tears" (2:4), and I wondered, "Can it actually be that Paul wept?" I read that he was "perplexed" (4:8), and I thought "Was Paul *really* perplexed?" And I read this: "We are weighed down exceedingly, beyond our power, so that we despaired even of life" (1:8); and I asked myself, amazed, "Is it possible that Paul even *despaired*?" It had never occurred to me that a person like Paul could have such experiences as these, but as I read on I gradually awakened to the fact that Christians are not another order of angelic beings, incapable of human feeling, and I saw that, after all, Paul was not so very remote from us. In fact, I discovered that Paul was *a man*, and the very sort of man I knew.

Numbers of people have their own conceptions of a Christian, but these conceptions are one-sided, because they are just a creation of the human mind; they are not a creation of God. In Paul I meet "this treasure," but, praise God, I also meet "an earthen vessel"! And this, I repeat, is the distinctive feature of Christianity, that "we have this treasure in earthen vessels." Here is a man who is afraid and yet determined; he is encompassed by foes and yet he is not bound; he seems about to be overcome and yet he is not destroyed. It is plain enough that he is weak, and yet he declares that just when he is weak he is strong. You can see that he bears in his body the dying of Jesus and yet he regards this as the very ground for the manifesting of the life of Jesus in his mortal body.

For appearances are not the whole story. Behind the man himself, and giving the lie to those appearances, there is the exceeding greatness of the power which is of God. Men may behold him "as deceiver, as unknown, as sorrowful, as poor, as having nothing, yes, as dying" even—and notwithstanding all this, God will support his bold assertion: "... and yet true, well-known, always rejoicing, making many rich, possessing all things: Behold we live!" (See 2 Cor. 6:8-10.)

POWER IN WEAKNESS

Do you begin now to understand what it means to be a Christian? To be a Christian is to be a person in whom seeming incompatibles exist together, but in whom it is the power of God that repeatedly triumphs. A Christian is one in whose life there is inherent a mysterious paradox, and this paradox is of God. Some people conceive of Christianity as being all treasure and no vessel. If sometimes the earthen vessel is evident in a servant of God, they feel he is a hopeless case, whereas God's conception is that, in that very vessel, his treasure should be found.

At this point we must distinguish carefully be-

tween man, and "the flesh" in man—between
the limitation that is inherent in our being
human at all, and the carnal nature of man with
its inveterate tendency to sin, a tendency that
leaves us (apart from the help of the Holy Spirit)
totally powerless to please God. This distinction
is the more important because of the ease with
which, even in a child of God, the one leads over
into the other, and human nature in us gives way
to carnal nature. Let it be quite clear, therefore,
that I certainly do not mean in this chapter to
excuse or condone sin or carnality. The flesh is
to be withstood and given over to death—the
death of the cross. (I have developed this theme
at greater length elsewhere.[2]) But weakness, in
this other sense, is to remain. Our blessed Lord
himself was for our sakes "crucified through
weakness," yet lives through the power of God
(2 Cor. 13:4); and as for ourselves, it is in our very
weakness that *his* power is to be made perfect.
There is therefore an "infirmity" in which it is
possible to glory (12:9).

So Paul tells us that he had "a thorn in the
flesh." What it was I do not know, but I do know
that it greatly weakened him, and that three
times he prayed for its removal. But for answer,
God only assured him: "My grace is sufficient for
thee." Only that—but that was enough.

How can the Lord's power be manifested to
perfection in a weak man? By Christianity; for
Christianity *is* that very thing. Christianity is not
the removal of weakness, nor is it merely the

[2]*The Normal Christian Life,* chapters 9 and 10.

manifestation of divine power. It is the manifestation of divine power *in the presence* of human weakness. Let us be clear on this point. What the Lord is doing is no merely negative thing—that is to say, the elimination of our infirmity. Nor, for that matter, is it merely positive—the bestowal of strength anywhere at random. No, he leaves us with the infirmity, and he bestows the strength *there*. He is bestowing his strength upon men, but that strength is manifested *in* their weakness. All the treasure he gives is placed in earthen vessels.

FAITH IN THE PRESENCE OF DOUBT

What we have just said is strikingly true of faith. Numbers of people have come to me and told of their fears and misgivings even while they have sought to trust the Lord. They have made their requests, they have laid hold of the promises of God, and yet doubts continually arise unbidden. Let me tell you, the treasure of true faith appears in a vessel that may be sorely assailed by doubt, and the earthen vessel, by its presence, does not nullify the treasure; rather does the treasure in such an environment shine forth with enhanced beauty. Do not misunderstand me, I am not encouraging doubt. Doubt is a mark of deficiency in a Christian; but I do wish to make this clear, that Christianity is not a matter of faith only, but of faith triumphing in the presence of doubt.

I love to recall the prayer of the early church for Peter's deliverance from the hands of wicked men. When Peter came back from the prison and knocked at the door where the church was at prayer, the believers exclaimed, "It is his angel." Do you see? There was faith there, true faith, the kind of faith that could bring an answer from God; and yet the weakness of man was still present, and doubt lurked just around the corner, as it were. But today the faith many of God's people claim to exercise is greater than that exercised by the believers gathered in the house of Mary the mother of John Mark. And they are so positive about it! They are certain God will send an angel, and that every door in the prison will swing open before him. If a gust of wind blows: "There's Peter knocking at the door!" If the rain begins to patter: "There's Peter knocking again!"

These people are too credulous, too cocksure. Their faith is not necessarily the genuine article. Even in the most devoted Christian, the earthen vessel is always there, and, at least to himself, it is always in evidence, though the determining factor is never the vessel but the treasure within. In the life of a normal Christian, just when faith rises positively to lay hold of God, a question may simultaneously arise as to whether perhaps he might be mistaken. When he is strongest in the Lord he is often most conscious of inability; when he is most courageous he may be most aware of fear within; and where he is most joyful a sense of distress readily enough breaks upon him again. Only the exceeding greatness of the power lifts him on high. But this paradox is itself evidence, both that there is a treasure, and that it is where God would have it be.

It must ever be a cause for great gratitude to God that no merely human weakness need limit divine power. We are apt to think that where sadness exists joy cannot exist; that where there are tears there cannot be praise; that where weakness is apparent power must be lacking; that when we are surrounded by foes we must be hemmed in; that where there is doubt there can be no faith. But let me proclaim strongly and with confidence that God is seeking to bring us to the point where everything human is only intended to provide an earthen vessel to contain the divine treasure. Henceforth, when we are conscious of depression, let us not give way to that depression but give way to the Lord; when doubt or fear arises in our hearts, let us not yield to these but to the Lord, and the treasure will shine forth all the more gloriously because of the earthen vessel.

JOY AMID PAIN

In the last of his letters, Paul writes to Timothy of the perils of the "last days." He warns them that grievous times will come, when men will be (among other things) *"without natural affection"* (2 Tim. 3:1-3). This is something of which we ought to take note. Here is a danger of the last days of this age—that men will have no feelings, no natural sensitivity, no human affections. This is, of course, a non-Christian state of affairs. An extreme example of it is that of a modern society of which I have heard, which, it is said, made one of the qualifications of its active agents that they should have killed one of their nearest and dearest. Yet these verses to Timothy are written for Christians, not for unbelievers. Are we to conclude, then, that this state of affairs will have invaded Christianity and be found among believers in the end times? It may be so, and that men will come to the place where they disclaim responsibility for parents, wives, or children, and *think that in so doing they are being good Christians.*

Of course, it is true that the Lord Jesus said: "If any man cometh unto me, and hateth not his own father, and mother, and wife, and children, and brethren, and sisters, yea, and his own life also, he cannot be my disciple" (Luke 14:25, 26). Yes, he said that, but he certainly did *not* say, as some even in our day have seemed to think, that only those who *rejoiced* to leave father and mother and wife and children could be disciples of his. In the name of service to the Lord, people have deserted their own kindred and dependents out of sheer heartlessness, and not out of love for him. "I am so spiritual," they say, "that I don't want anything to do with my family." I knew a Chinese brother who claimed to be very devoted to the Lord because he did not mind leaving his family and going off to serve him in the gospel, when all of us knew that, as a matter of fact, he had never truly cared for them. This kind of thing is all too common, and God has no place for it.

True spirituality is to *care*, but yet to let the Cross of Christ deal with the things that stand in the way of the will of God. That is to say, we go forth because the Lord calls us, and not because we are glad of an easy escape from our home responsibilities. It is a fairly safe rule that if there is *no cost* in going forth for him, something is wrong and the move is not a spiritual move. There is a place for the family life to be sanctified and held in honor *and yet* for the natural strength in us of the carnal life and affections to be touched and dealt with by God.

For remember again, God looks for the treasure *in the vessel.* Here is Christianity, not that we camouflage the vessel by steeling ourselves to suppress all feeling, but that we let the earthen vessel be seen with the treasure inside. It is not a case of getting through painful situations because one has become insensible to pain, but of retaining full consciousness and being carried through by Another, despite the feeling of pain. The earthen vessel is there, but the treasure is also there. What is the treasure? It is the life of the Lord Jesus—the triumphant life of him who "wept" and "groaned within himself," and who "sighed deeply in his spirit" and was "exceeding sorrowful, even unto death" (See John 11:33, 35, 38; 12:27; 13:21; Mark 8:12; Matt. 26:37, 38).

Yes, our humanity is an earthen vessel. Wherein, then, do we differ as Christians from other vessels? Not by any difference in the material of the vessel, but by the difference of its content. The only thing that distinguishes us is the miracle of the treasure enshrined within.

I knew a brother who was very attached to his wife. On one occasion it had been arranged that he should go on a preaching tour that would keep him away from home for some months, and it happened that, at the time he was due to leave, his wife was in poor health, having been confined only six days before. A friend sent me with a letter to him, and as I turned into his street and drew near his house, he came out with a man carrying his luggage. I saw him, but he did not see me. I watched him come out and walk a little distance, then stop and look back at his house, and then after a little hesitation begin to return slowly. I did not wait longer, but sensing some conflict in his spirit I went ahead to the riverboat by another route, as I did not wish to intrude by going down with him. When he arrived at the boat I said to him, "Brother, may the Lord bless you." He seemed quite happy, and replied, "Yes, may the Lord indeed bless us."

When after some months he came back from the tour, I asked him if he remembered the incident, explaining what I had seen without his noticing me. He said: "Of course I remember. It was just six days after the birth of the baby; my wife had no servant, and there were the two other little children to look after. Added to that, I had not been able to leave much money with her. As I stood there I felt I *could* not leave her like that; it was cruel to do so. But as I was retracing my steps that verse came to me: 'No man, having put his hand to the plow, and looking back, is fit for the kingdom of God.' So I turned again, and went down to the boat."

I like to tell that story, because it illustrates so clearly what is the earthen vessel and what is the treasure within. "Your body is a temple of the

Holy Ghost which is in you" (1 Cor. 6:19). That is the Christian life. Some people do not seem to have any earthen vessel; they are disembodied spirits, not human beings—or at least that is what they try to be! But to hold on to the plow while wiping our tears—this is Christianity. It is the transcending of the earthen vessel by the treasure within.

ANGER WITHOUT SIN

Finally, I want to apply this principle practically along a rather different line. For Scripture occasionally indicates a positive sense in which this duality of our existence on earth—the human vessel and the spiritual life planted within it by new birth—should operate. In Ephesians 4:26, 27 the apostle Paul says: "Be ye angry, and sin not." What do we know of this? Of course, to get angry and sin is always wrong; but how many of us think that the only way to avoid sinning is not to get angry! We simply do not know *how* to get angry and yet not sin.

Here again it is most helpful to look at the humanity of the Lord Jesus. When he crossed the sea with the disciples in the storm, we read that they were afraid and cried out. What did the Lord do? He did not just help them in their need; we read that he also rebuked them, saying: "Why are ye fearful, O ye of little faith?" (Matt. 8:26). I am glad the Lord could feel things strongly and could speak such plain words. How many saints throughout the centuries have been helped by that challenge! Again, when the disciples brought to Jesus the lunatic boy, he said: "O faithless and perverse generation, how long shall I be with you? How long shall I bear with you?" (Matt. 17:17). How many of us have been stirred too by these words to seek to learn the lesson of that incident!

To the Pharisees, when the occasion demanded, he could speak with tremendous force: "Woe unto you, ye blind guides!" "Ye have made void the word of God because of your tradition. Ye hypocrites!" (Matt. 15:6; 23:16 ff.). And when he went into the temple and cast out those that sold and bought, and overthrew the tables of the moneychangers, it was said of him: "The zeal of thy house hath eaten me up" (John 2:17). He was stirred with indignation. But alas, how few Christians know that Spirit-controlled stirring within that the Lord knew, and consequently, how few know anything of the spiritual authority that accompanied it! Yet there was no contradiction in him. He could declaim: "Woe unto thee, Chorazin! Woe unto thee, Bethsaida!" and yet we read that, at that very season (and without inconsistency), "He rejoiced in the Holy Spirit, and said, I thank thee, O Father, Lord of heaven and earth" (Luke 10:13, 21; cf. Matt. 11:20-25).

The point is this, that there exists for Christians an anger which is apart from sin, and yet even sincere Christians often do not understand how to distinguish sin from anger and so they cast both away. There are many things in the world which ought to be rebuked, but how many really know how to administer that rebuke?

Alas, very few. We have lost that power. To clap a man on the shoulder when he is wrong, while turning a blind eye to his deeds for the sake of his friendship, is a cheap way out. To rebuke him may be costly, but the Lord may require it of us.

Why can we not rebuke? Because almost always, in doing so, we expose ourselves in turn to rebuke, for we do not know how to get angry without yielding to sin. We are not truly under the Holy Spirit's constraint in this as we should be. Indeed many of us have not gone the way that makes that constraint possible. For anger that is without sin is always costly, presupposing as it does God's initial dealing with us by the Cross. In our own thoughts and emotions (as we are by nature, and apart from the Spirit of God), sin and anger are indeed inseparable, for unlike that of the Lord Jesus, our humanity is a fallen humanity, our flesh a sinful flesh. In us there is a basic contradiction where in him there was none, and if we yield to anger we shall surely sin.

Yet to be angry without committing sin is not only a possibility; it is a command. "Be ye angry, and sin not; let not the sun go down upon your wrath: neither give place to the devil" (Eph. 4:26, 27). Implied in these words is one secret of being angry and yet not sinning, namely, to see that we do not sustain our anger until the evening. In other words *we* are not to enter into it. If we harbor wrath after the event, it is evidence that the thing has touched *us*; and when *we* are touched by it, then be sure there is sin. So here God has set for us a helpful time limit: we may be stirred to wrath, but we are not to allow the sun to go down upon it. Anger can be free from sin when, being full of anger, we are yet under divine control, so that when the time comes for the anger to stop, it stops. It is when *we* enter in and take hold that anger cannot be stopped.

Most of the Lord's children know that anger is a human emotion, and when justifiably angry they know that it is wrong to give way to it by letting it be prolonged. In spite of this there are, sadly enough, all too many who repeatedly give it rein and let their emotions get quite out of control. But at the other extreme are some who have sought escape from the problem by trying to suppress all natural emotion in themselves. Things can go past such people, and they contrive to remain aloof and quite untouched by them. Now of course, the first of these extremes we can justly see reason to blame, but we do not so easily see that the second also is a too easy escape from responsibility. We are not meant, by gripping tight on to ourselves, to suppress all human emotion until we end up frigid as ice. Indeed those who achieve that state are a constant drain on others around them, who must somehow make good from their side the deficiency in "natural affection" if relationships are to remain even reasonably comfortable. No, we must rather allow God's Holy Spirit to make his own use of our emotions and powers of expression. Of course it is true that *he* must be in command. Of course we must *have* the divine treasure—yes, but not in cold storage! We need, along with it, the simple earthen vessel that should contain it and through which it should express itself.

To be angry and sin, is sin; but I repeat, there *is* an anger that is without sin. We can be angry and yet have love in our hearts. It is perfectly possible to be aroused to anger and yet to weep for those towards whom that anger is stirred. Paul could weep, but he could still be firm. "I made you sorry with my epistle," he writes. "Who is made to stumble, and I burn not?" And again: "If I come again, I will not spare" (2 Cor. 7:8; 11:29; 13:2). God wants that earthen vessel, not covered or camouflaged, but *controlled by the treasure.*

Herein lies the glory of Christianity, that God's treasure can be manifest in every humblest vessel of clay. Christianity is a paradox, and it is as we Christians live this paradoxical life that we get to know God. Indeed, the further we go on in the Christian life the more paradoxical it becomes. The treasure becomes increasingly manifest, but the earthen vessel is the earthen vessel still. This is very beautiful. See the divine patience in a man who by nature was impatient, and compare the sight of that with a man whom nothing could ever move. See the divine humility in one who was by nature haughty, and compare that with one who was always of a retiring disposition. See the strength of God in a person of weak temperament, and compare that with a naturally strong character. The difference is immeasurable.

People who are naturally weak are apt to underrate their value to the Lord, just because of the very evident earthenness of their vessel. But

where is the ground for dejection, when the
treasure within is of such a nature as to acquire
added splendor from the very fact that it shines
forth from such a vessel? Brothers and sisters, let
me say once again, the whole question is one of
the quality of the treasure, not of the deficiencies
of the vessel that contains it. It is folly to stress
the negative side; our concern is with the positive. There are some Christians of whom we can
readily see that they are quick or slow, fearful or
impulsive, credulous or impatient, by nature.
Yet—and this is the miracle—there is at the same
time present in them a precious treasure which,
because the mark of the Cross is upon their
human frailty, shines triumphantly through it
all. The exceeding greatness of the power is not
of ourselves—but of God.

5
God's sure Foundation

The autobiographical sections in 2 Corinthians have brought to our attention an aspect of the Christian's personal walk with his Lord that is there thrown into relief by the apostle's account of his experiences as a minister of the gospel. Coming now to what we regard as the peculiar and characteristic element in Paul's ministry, we will begin by turning back to his letter to the Romans, and especially to its later sections. Chapter 12 of that letter opens with an appeal to us to present ourselves as servants to the will of

God. Such a consecration is the "reasonable" outcome of all that he has said up to that point, both as to personal faith and divine election. Immediately upon that, we find him alluding to "the Body of Christ," and this term best covers the topic of study immediately before us. "We are one body in Christ," he says, "and severally members one of another." What does he mean?

From eternity there has been, he explains, something held in the very heart of God, which the incarnate Son of God was anointed to bring to realization. He speaks of it as a "mystery"—that is to say, a divine secret, held in reserve through the ages and only now made known by God to his servants through "the preaching of Jesus Christ" in this new day of the Spirit (Rom. 16:25, 26). Its unfolding presents us with a fundamental difference between our idea of salvation and God's—between our conception of the redemptive work of the Cross and the full divine conception.

As we said above in speaking of chapters 1-8 of Romans, we all of us believe that the Cross of Christ is central to the whole work of God, and we praise God for making this fact clear to our hearts. But we must remember that the Cross was and is a means to an end, never an end in itself. The divine end to which it is intended to lead is this that Paul terms "the Body of Christ." If we know the Cross in the way in which God means it to be known, we shall inevitably find ourselves within the Body. It cannot be otherwise. If we are not there in spirit, we shall have to confess that in us the Cross has as yet done only a part of its transforming work.

Salvation, forgiveness, justification, deliverance, personal holiness, victorious living, walking after the Spirit: all these most precious fruits of redemption are ours to enjoy, but they are not meant to apply to us merely as so many myriads of separate units, scattered over this earth for God. Their values are intended to go further than that. Salvation is in terms of the Body, deliverance is in terms of the Body, personal holiness is in terms of the Body. It may be true that the children of Abraham are as the sand of the seashore in multitude. Nevertheless, as Christians, God would have us see ourselves not as men but as a Man. The goal of the divine thought is in fact one heavenly Man, not a host of little men.

One day, I confess, I could not resist saying this in answer to a questioner when I was preaching the gospel in a Chinese village. A scholar had been listening attentively, and after a while remarked, "Mr. Nee, you preach your religion to bring us poor sinners to heaven; but I do not think *I* will get in there at all. It will be far too crowded!" In the circumstances, my reply to this was hardly a fair one, and looking back I fear that, apart from the Spirit's help, its point must have been largely lost on him. "You are wrong," I said. "Heaven will never be crowded. Throughout heaven there will only be one Man, not two, and certainly not a crowd! The only Man in heaven is God's one new Man—God's Son himself and those who by faith are in him. *That* is where he wants you!" And of course that is true. God views his people not as unrelated units but as that one heavenly Man: Christ the Head, and we the members. This was the discovery the apostle Paul had made.

He does not tell us how this new revelation of Christ came to him. Indeed, though he was a man of deep experience and of much secret history with God, it is remarkable that he keeps very quiet about the nature and means of his "visions and revelations of the Lord." It would not be profitable, he said, for him to boast of them, and only against his desires and under strong compulsion of circumstances did he speak of the visions of "a man in Christ, fourteen years ago" (2 Cor. 12:1, 2). Fourteen years! And yet with many of us, directly we have something from God, the whole of Shanghai knows it! To suppress it even for two years would be a feat. But Paul, even after fourteen years, does not tell us *what* that vision was, save that it was a further revelation of Jesus Christ. What is clear, however, is that it made a deep impression on him, and there is no doubt that what he saw came out in practical terms in his ministry.

THE CROSS AND THE BODY

"Now in Christ Jesus ye ... are made nigh by the blood of Christ. For he is our peace, who made both [Jew and Gentile] one ... that he might create in himself of the twain one new man ... and might reconcile them both in one body unto God through the cross" (See Eph. 2:11-22). What, we must ask ourselves, is this "one body," this "one new man"? What is this mystery of Christ that Paul has come to see?

In Romans 6:6 he has spoken of "our old man," by which he means everything that comes to us from "the first man, Adam"; and he sees this "old man" as having been nailed to the cross with Christ. In Colossians 3:11, 12 he speaks of "the new man" as the sphere where now "there cannot be Greek and Jew ... but Christ is all and in all." For our old man there was only crucifixion with Christ; in the new Man we are found in union with him, risen and ascended. Between the one and the other towers the Cross as the only gateway into this fellowship with one another in Jesus Christ.

You ask me, what do I mean when I use the term "the Cross" in this way? I think it is best summed up in the words the crowd used of its Victim: "Away with him!" Crucifixion humanly speaking, is an end. The Cross of Christ is intended by God to be, first of all, the end of everything in man that has come under his sentence of death, for there it was that he took our place, and the judgment of God was fulfilled upon him.

But the Cross has a further value for us, for it is there also that the Christian believer's self-sufficient and individualistic natural life is broken, as Jacob's strength and independence of nature were broken at Jabbok. There comes a day in God's dealings with each of us when we suffer in our souls that incapacitating wound, and ever afterwards "go halting." God never allows this to remain for us a mere theory. Alas, I must confess that for many years it *was* no more than theory to me. I myself had "preached the Cross" in this very sense, yet without knowing anything of it in my own experience—until one day I *saw* that it had been I, Nee To-sheng, who died there with Christ. "Away with him!" they had said, and in saying it they unwittingly echoed God's verdict upon *my* old man. And that sentence upon me was carried out *in him*. This tremendous discovery affected me almost as greatly as did my first discovery of salvation. I tell you, it left me for seven whole months so humbled as to be quite unable to preach at all, whereas for long, I have to confess, preaching had been my consuming passion.

But if to see this somewhat negative aspect of the Cross can be so drastic an experience, it is not surprising that its positive aspect—the revelation to our hearts of the heavenly Body of Christ—has proved for many to be no less revolutionary. For it is like suddenly finding yourself in a place which you have hitherto known only by hearsay. And how different the reality proves! Reading a guide to London is no substitute for visiting that city. Nor can a book of recipes take the place of a spell of work in the kitchen. To know anything experimentally, we must sooner or later find ourselves personally involved in it.

Yes, there are certain fundamental experiences we must have, and this "seeing" of the Body of Christ, the heavenly Man is one such. What is it? It is simply a discovery of values that, as I have said, lie on the resurrection side of the Cross. There, what has been for us already a way of release *from* our old selfish "natural life" in

Adam becomes the gateway *into* the new, shared "everlasting life" in Christ. For unlike other Roman crucifixions, the Cross of Christ is not just an end; it is also a beginning. In his death and resurrection, our disunion gives way to oneness of life in him.

God is not satisfied with single, separate Christians. When we believed on the Lord and partook of him we became members of his Body. Oh that God would cause this fact to break upon us! Do I seek spiritual experiences for myself? Do I make converts for my denomination? Or have I caught the wisdom of the one heavenly Man, and realized that God is seeking to bring men into that? When I do, salvation, deliverance, enduement with the Spirit, yes, everything in Christian experience will be seen from a new viewpoint, everything for me will be transformed.

We shall now seek to develop some aspects of this subject further. In the New Testament we find the Church variously described, as a spiritual house or temple ("a habitation of God through the Spirit"), as a body or a man ("the Body of Christ," "one new man"), and as a wife ("a bride adorned for her husband"), and we must keep these analogies in mind in what follows. In the remainder of this chapter we shall speak of the Church's foundation, and then, in four subsequent chapters, we shall touch in turn upon her eternal character, her fellowship, her ministries, and her present high calling and task. We shall not, even then, have finished with this matter of the Church, for so great is its significance to God that, when we come to the ministry

of the apostle John, we cannot fail to see the large
place it takes at the end.

UPON THIS ROCK

"According to the grace of God which was
given unto me, as a wise masterbuilder I laid a
foundation," writes Paul to the Corinthians.
What was this foundation of which he speaks? It
was certainly nothing peculiar to Paul, nor did it
originate with him. It was something which the
apostles had in common, and we must turn back
briefly to the Gospels and to the words of the
Lord Jesus himself for a first definition of it. Hear
him at Caesarea Philippi, as he addresses Simon
Peter in these remarkable terms: "Thou art Peter,
and upon this rock I will build my church"
(Matt. 16:18).

It is important to understand this passage, for
as we shall see, it really defines the point from
which, later, Paul in his turn begins. What did
Jesus imply? Thou art *Petros,* a stone—one who
is to be builded with others into the basic structure of my Church (see Eph. 2:20; Rev. 21:19)—
and on this Rock I will build. What then is the
Church? It is a structure of living stones founded
upon a rock. And what is the rock? Here it is that
we need to be very clear. It is a *confession* based
upon a *revelation* of a *Person.*

Jesus, who never seemed to care what men
said or thought about him, suddenly put the
question to his disciples: "Who do men say that
I, the Son of Man, am?" Then, turning from the
views and speculations of others, he went a step

further: "Who say ye that I am?" His challenge drew forth spontaneously from Peter the historic confession: "*Thou art the Christ, the Son of the living God.*" Thus it is true to say that the Church is built upon a confession, for to "say" is to confess, not merely to hazard an opinion. Moreover it was no empty confession such as might today be based on study or deduction or "point of view." As Jesus made clear, Peter's confession was called forth by a God-given revelation. "Flesh and blood hath not revealed it unto thee, but my Father which is in heaven." And further, it was a revelation of the true character and meaning of Jesus, and not merely of facts about him—not merely, that is, of what the Gospels tell us he did, but of what and who he is. As to his person, he is the Son of the living God; as to his office and ministry, he is the Christ. All this was contained in Peter's words.

This dual discovery was later, as we have said, to become Paul's starting point. Read again, for example, his opening words to the Romans. The Jesus whom he had persecuted is now, he affirms, "declared the Son of God with power, according to the spirit of holiness, by the resurrection of the dead; even Jesus Christ our Lord" (Rom. 1:4). All he writes to the churches is founded upon this revelation concerning Jesus. From everlasting to everlasting he is the Son of God: that is the first thing. But there came a day when, taking upon himself the form of a servant, he became also the Christ, the Anointed One, God's Minister. All God's purpose, all God's hopes are bound up with that risen Christ. It is he who has been separated and anointed as God's sure foundation.

But if he is the foundation, we are the living stones. To recognize Christ is to recognize also the Christians, and God's plan through them for the universe. For we shall be of little use to God if we know only our salvation, and have caught no glimpse of the purpose for which he has brought us into relation to his Son. How many claim to have the anointing of the Spirit, and yet seem quite unaware that the object for which the Spirit is given to Christ and to his members is one and the same! It is directed to one and the same divine end. To see this is suddenly to see the extreme smallness of all our work that in the past has been unrelated to that end.

Let us be clear about this fact, that the Church is not merely a company of people whose sins are forgiven and who are going to heaven; it is a company of those whose eyes have been opened by God to recognize the person and work of the Son. This is something far more than man can see or know or handle—far more, even, than the outward experiences of those disciples who for three years, as his constant companions, ate and slept, walked and lived with him. Truly theirs was a great happiness, and how many of us would not gladly exchange places with Peter for a few days? But even their experience did not unite them with him as a part of the Church. Only revelation from God as to who Christ is can do that to you and me. The Rock is Christ—yes, but a revealed Christ not a theoretical or doctrinal Christ. Twenty years among Christians and a lifetime of exercise in theology will not build us into his Church. It is inner, not outer knowledge that brings that about. "This is life eternal, that they should know thee the only true God, and him whom thou didst send, even Jesus Christ" (John 17:3).

"No man knoweth who the Son is save the Father" (Luke 10:22). Flesh and blood cannot know the man God has established. Yet he must be known, for the Church's foundation is not only Christ but the knowledge of Christ. And the tragedy today is that many in the churches—indeed many so-called churches—lack such foundation. But theory will not prevail against hell, which is what Jesus declares his Church must do. Have we perhaps forgotten what we are for? Visiting Western homes I have sometimes seen a beautiful porcelain plate, not put to use on the table but wired and hung up to the wall as an ornament. It seems to me that many think of the Church rather like that, as something to be admired for the perfection of its form and pattern. But no, God's Church is for use, not decoration. Head-knowledge, instruction, order, may produce an appearance of life when conditions are favorable, but when the gates of hell come out against us they all too soon disclose to us our true state. Very many saw, followed, pressed upon, were touched and healed by Jesus, but did not know him. Yet to one who followed, these words were said: "On this Rock I will build." We may think we are just as good as—even possibly a little better than—Peter. He was tempted and fell. Yes, but was he not better in his fall than many who never do so? He denied—but he could weep. For he *knew*. Many do not fall, but neither do they know.

It is first-hand knowledge that counts in the hour of testing. I do not mean that members of the Church should not help each other, but what is merely passed on from man to man is of little use if there be, with it, no revelation from heaven. It will not stand the fire. That is why in our word for a martyr, *hsuin taochoe*, "one slain for a doctrine," I think *tao* is wrong, for who ever dies for a doctrine? At one time I used to fear lest a modernist should come along and prove to me that the Bible was unreliable, and with it therefore the historic facts in which my faith was founded. If he did, I thought, that would finish everything; and I *wanted* to believe. But now everything is peaceful. If men were to bring as many arguments as there are shells in the armories of Europe, it would make not the least difference to me—for I know! The knowledge we get from men may deceive us. At best it is imperfect, and however good it be, we may forget it. But the Father revealed the Son he knew to Peter. This revelation is Christianity. There is no Church without it. I, from within, recognize Jesus as Son of God, and as Christ—that is the heart of everything. The response of Jesus to Peter was not "You have answered correctly" but "God has shown that to you!"

Thus the Rock defines the limits of the Church. They extend wherever such a confession goes up to God from the heart—there and no further. For remember, this was not a general

confession; it sprang from revelation. And not
from a general revelation either, but one that
concerned a Man, the Son of man. Nothing
gives God greater satisfaction than confession
of himself. Jesus often said, "I am." He loves to
hear us say, "Thou art." We do it far too little.
"Thou art Lord!" When everything goes wrong
and all is confusion, don't pray, but confess
that Jesus is Lord. Today, when the world is in
turmoil, stand and proclaim that Jesus is King
of kings and Lord of lords. He loves to hear us
say what we *know*. The Church is not only
founded on revelation but on confession—on
our speaking out what we know of God. The
Church today is Christ's voice set down here
upon the earth.

If God has not opened our eyes to see that
death is the power, the weapon, of the gates of
hell, we shall scarcely know the value of
speaking out. But when suddenly, in some
hitherto unforeseen circumstance, we find to
our alarm that apparently faith does not work,
prayer does not work, we shall learn the need
to proclaim Christ, and in doing so shall discover what it was God was waiting for. "Thou
art Lord. Thou art Victor. Thou art King." The
best prayer of all is not "I want" but "Thou
art." By the revelation given to us, let us speak.
In prayer meetings, at the Breaking of Bread,
alone before the Lord, in the midst of the
thronging world, or in the dark hour of need,
learn to proclaim, "Thou art." This is the
Church's voice, God's voice in the earth, the
voice that, above all else, hell fears.

HEAVENLY WISDOM

The apostle Paul stands in the main stream of a long line of men to whom God was pleased to make known something of his purpose. "Shall I hide from Abraham that which I do?" "Joseph dreamed a dream, and he told it to his brethren: and they hated him..." "Gather yourselves together, that I [Jacob] may tell you that which shall befall you in the latter days." "According to all that I show thee [Moses] ... even so shall ye make it." "All this, said David, have I been made to understand in writing from the hand of the Lord, even all the works of this pattern." "Blessed art thou, Simon Bar-Jonah: for flesh and blood hath not revealed it unto thee, but my Father which is in heaven." "By revelation was made known unto me [Paul] ... the mystery of Christ, which ... hath now been revealed unto his holy apostles and prophets in the Spirit." "I shrank not from declaring unto you the whole counsel of God." (Gen. 18:17; 37:5; 49:1; Ex. 25:9; 1 Chr. 28:19; Matt. 16:17; Eph. 3:3; Acts 20:27.) None of these men came into the work of God by the exercise of their wits, for all God's work is related to his eternal purpose in Christ, and that purpose can only be known by divine unveiling. What a difficulty this presents for clever people!

Of the many typical servants of God in the Old Testament, Joseph is perhaps the most perfect. Yet, while Scripture reveals no apparent flaw in his character, we know well that his was no easy pathway. When did his troubles begin? Surely with his dreams. In them he saw what God was going to do, and recognized his own place in God's plan. It was his dreams that started things off. They represent spiritual vision. By them he saw what his brothers could not see. "This dreamer cometh," they said, and hated him. But because he saw, Joseph could stand fast through all those grim experiences, and by him God was able to fulfill his plan for his earthly people.

By the time Moses appeared the nation was formed, but still of course in Egypt. God raised him up to bring them out, and he was shown what God would do to relate them as a people to himself as the center of their life. Moses saw the pattern in the Mount. In due course Israel's whole life would come to revolve around that Tabernacle and the divine Presence in their midst. Thus Moses dedicated himself to build, not according to his own ideas—he dare not do that—but, as with Joseph, according to what he *saw*. For vision is not our opinion as to what God should do; it is *seeing* what he is going to do.

Where does the work of God begin? On his side its starting-point is in eternity past; on ours it is the point at which we receive revelation of Christ. The start of a true work of God with us is not when we consecrate ourselves to him, but when we *see*. Consecration should result *from* spiritual vision; it can never take its place. That is where God's work begins. Our work may begin at any time; God's work through us can spring only from divinely given vision.

We must see his goal in Christ. Without that vision our service for God follows the impulse of our own ideas but cannot accord with God's

plan. When we come to Paul, we see that for him
this revelation was twofold. "It pleased God ... to
reveal his Son in me": that was inner revelation,
subjective, if you like the term (Gal. 1:15 f.). "I
was not disobedient unto the heavenly vision";
that was outer vision, objective, concrete, practical (Acts 26:19). The inner and the outer together
make perfect completeness, whereas either is in-
sufficient without the other. And this is the need
of the Church, of the people of God, today. Inward revelation must go along with outward vision: not only knowing the Lord within, but
knowing also God's eternal purpose; not stopping at the foundation, but understanding too
how to build upon it. God is not satisfied with
our just doing odds and ends of work; that is
what servants do. We are his friends, and his
friends should know his plans.

What called forth Paul's consecration of himself was that flash of light from heaven. The
obedience sprang from the vision. For while it
remains true that all self-committal to God is
precious to him, blind self-committal does not
serve him very far. There is I think a difference
between the initial, pure but uninstructed consecration that follows conversion and the further
consecration of ourselves that may follow a seeing of the plan of God. The one is individual,
based on our salvation, and God may not at once
make severe demands upon it. But when God
reveals his need and shows us what he wants
done, and when having done so he asks for our
willingness and receives our response, then it is
that his demands upon that consecration become

intensified. We have given our word on the basis of a new understanding, and he takes us anew at our word. Praise God that, to the ever-increasing vision given to him, Paul was not disobedient. All he had went into it.

Vision of God's purpose today brings into view all the people of God, but it is also *for* all the people of God. That was not always so. What the Old Testament saints saw, great as it was, concerned only an earthly people, however typical they might be of the heavenly Church. And only chosen men such as Joseph and Moses were entrusted with that vision. It was not common property, but was only given to the few. Today, however, it is different. Heavenly vision now is for the whole Church. Though it is true that Paul and others in the New Testament period were chosen of God in a special way, his purpose is not that the vision should be confined to the ones and twos, but that all should see (Eph. 1:18). This is the special character of this age.

In an important passage in Ephesians 3, Paul writes to "you Gentiles" of the "dispensation of that grace of God which was given me to you-ward." He tells them of the "mystery of Christ" made known to him and to others by revelation (verses 2-5). This "manifold wisdom of God," he goes on to explain, has God planned even now to make known through his Church to all spiritual observers (verses 10, 11). To this end it must therefore first of all become her possession, and Paul's own part in this, he says, is governed by a single object, namely, *"to make all men see"* (verse 9).

Put in a sentence, the grace of God was given to the apostle that through his labors *the Church might see the vision.* For though Paul's "all men" embraces each member, the full revelation of God does not belong to the individual as such. What is to be made known through the Church can only be seen by the Church. It is "with all saints" that we apprehend the measure of the love of Christ. Only so can we be filled unto all the fullness of God (Eph. 3:18, 19).

THE PRECIOUSNESS OF LIGHT

So while nothing can take the place of vision, the problem is still to get men to see. It was the subject of the apostle's most earnest prayer (Eph. 1:15-18). There is no difficulty about hearing, or even memorizing and repeating to others the plan of God; the difficulty is always to see. And all spiritual work is based on seeing. However much God in his grace may bless what originates otherwise—and he does do so—it is but odds and ends. It is vulnerable. That is why Satan does not much mind men hearing about the purpose of God and understanding it mentally. His great fear is lest they should have inward illumination concerning that purpose. He knows that if they do they will have a new access of strength and power, and that the Church, the work, the warfare—everything will be seen by them in a fresh light.

What is vision? It is the breaking in of divine light. The veiling of that light means perdition.

"If our gospel is veiled, it is veiled in them that are perishing" (2 Cor. 4:3). But "God hath shined in our hearts"—and merely to *see* is salvation. As soon as we see the glory in the Savior's face, in that instant we are saved. If we merely understand the doctrine and assent to it, nothing happens, for we have not *seen* the Truth. But the moment we really see *him*, in that moment we have the experience.

This is true both negatively and positively, as to sin and as to the Savior. Before conversion men talk about the doctrine of the wrong of lying. They see it in the Word, they know the Word says it is wrong, and they may even make an effort to conform to that Word. And yet they lie, and lie well! Then one day they are converted. There is no immediate advance in their *doctrine* about lying, but at once they see that lying is wrong without being told. With a new instinct, they shrink with horror from the habit that till now had gripped them. What has happened? Light has made manifest its true nature, and the light that makes manifest is the light that slays. The light that reveals the lie slays the lie. What was till now merely an ethic has become an inward experience. And the experience, like that of salvation itself, follows the shedding of light within as instantaneously as the impression of a photograph in a camera follows the exposure of the film. The instant you open the shutter you get a portrait. And the vision of God's purpose, of what he wants to do in the Church, is of a like character, and no less revolutionary in its effect. But because it concerns not merely the individual but the whole plan of God in Christ, its implications are so much the greater. It is capable, as we have said, of transforming our whole conception of the service of God.

I am not suggesting that we shall start to upheave and overthrow the work that till now we have been doing for him. God forbid! Simply to change outward things is no use. We cannot deal with and improve things which God does not approve, nor dare we risk overthrowing that of which he does. No, the light kills *in us* all that is not of God, without any need of our doing violence to outward things. It is not a question of our grasping things mentally and getting to grips with them. There are some things we cannot grasp. It is all a question of seeing or not seeing. The whole issue is one of alternatives: light or darkness, life or death. Were it merely a matter of doctrine we might dismiss it from our mind and soon forget it. But objective, heavenly vision becomes also "his Son revealed in me"—the two are one—and there is no need to remember, or possibility of forgetting, that which lives. There is no need to hold on to or try to grasp spiritual vision. *It* lays hold of *us*. To see the plan of God from within is to have no alternative in work or way. Henceforth it is his way, or it is death.

If we want light, we can have it. In order not to have it we must shut it out. Of course this can be done, for someone has truly said that the smallest leaf can hide a star. We may let a trivial obstacle veil from us eternal glories. But given the slightest chance, light will find its way in through the tiniest chink. "If therefore thine eye

be single, thy whole body shall be full of light"
(Matt. 6:22).

The secret of spiritual vision is a readiness for
the cost of it, which means a humble openness of
spirit to the searching light of God. "The meek
will he guide in judgment; and the meek will he
teach his way. The secret of the Lord is with
them that fear him; and he will show them his
covenant" (Psalm 25:9, 14). "Lord, I am willing
to pay any price to receive light. I do not fear
light. I am willing for thee to search every cranny
of my work and to shed upon it the light of thine
own purpose."

As we go further with these studies, I hope
some of the vastness of God's purpose in the
Church will become apparent to us. But that is
not enough. My prayer, my longing, is that we
may see Christ in fullness. It is not sufficient that
we seek hereafter to build up, according to Scriptural doctrines, a good, earnest church as men
reckon it. No, *light* is our cry. We dare to face the
light. "Lord, give me, like Stephen, to see the
Son of man in heaven, and in his light to see
what thy Church is, thy work is. And then grant
me grace, not only to live and walk, but also to
work, in the light." The outstanding feature of
God's work is not a doctrine but a life; and life
comes by revelation in the light of God. Behind
doctrine there may be nothing but words. Behind revelation is God himself.

6
A Glorious Church

Introducing the subject of his Church, Jesus brings us straight to the Rock. He himself is the "precious corner stone of sure foundation" (Isa. 28:16). Each child of God who has life and is redeemed by his blood stands upon this foundation, and upon it he builds. Unbelievers have no part here at all. Whether it be the Church universal or its local expression, the principle is one and the same: Christ is the "tried stone" to whom we are brought and fashioned and fitted.

Paul too takes this as his point of departure, for

certainly it is the only possible one. "We are ...
God's building," he writes to the Corinthians in
one of his letters, and then goes on: "As a wise
masterbuilder I laid a foundation ... But let each
man take heed how he buildeth thereon. For
other foundation can no man lay than that which
is laid, which is Jesus Christ" (1 Cor. 3:9-11). In
other words the choice of a foundation is no
longer our responsibility. God himself has laid
it, and no man can lay any other; no man can
begin anywhere else. The apostles witness to
this, and God does not ask our approval! He has
done it, and he knows what he is doing.
Whenever a soul comes to Christ, and Christ en-
ters into the life, that foundation is laid. On it the
child of God stands, on it he builds. What does
matter, however, is what he puts on it.

God looks for quality. He is not concerned so
much with whether we do the work as with what
we use to do it. Many argue, "If my work is well
done, surely that is enough!" But God asks not
merely whether we have served him, given ourselves to his work, and built on the foundation,
important though these things are. His question
goes deeper. What, he inquires, have we used to
do these things? He looks, not only at the things
done, but at the materials used. Among those
who preach the Gospel he is aware of a difference of quality, and readily distinguishes the
solid from the superficial worker. Among those
who see spiritual truth he recognizes a like difference in their seeing. Among those who pray
he discerns what lies behind each one's
"Amen." This is what Paul means when he

warns us: "If any man buildeth on the foundation gold, silver, costly stones, wood, hay, stubble; each man's work shall be made manifest: for the day shall declare it, because it is revealed in fire" (verses 12, 13).

MATERIAL FOR BUILDING

It is weight that counts. Wood, hay, stubble are cheap, light, temporary; gold, silver, precious stones are costly, weighty, eternal. Here is the key to value. The heavy metals, the gold of the divine character and glory, the silver of his redemptive work: these are the materials he prizes. Not merely what we preach, but what we are, weighs with God; not doctrine, but the character of Christ wrought out in us by God's orderings, by God's testings, by the Spirit's patient workings. Work that is of God is work that has been to the Cross. When our work has been that way, we can rest assured that it will in the end survive the fire. Not, "Where is the need most evident? What ideas and resources have I got? How much can I do? How soon can I put that doctrine into practice?" but, "Where is God moving? What is there of him here? How far is it his will for me to go? What is the mind of the Spirit on this?"—these are the questions of the truly crucified servant. He recognizes God's "Go" and his "Speak," but also his "Wait," and his "Go, but say only so much." Aware of his own weakness and emptiness, his greatest lesson is to commit his way to God and learn to see him move.

The problem lies in our failure to understand

that, in God's work, man in himself is of no use. Wood, hay, stubble, these suggest what is essentially of man and of the flesh. They imply what is common, ordinary, easily and cheaply acquired—and of course perishable. Grass today may clothe the earth with beauty, but where is it tomorrow? Human intellect may give us a grasp of Scripture; natural eloquence may have the power to attract; emotion may carry us along; feelings may seem to supply a guiding sense— but to what? God looks for more solid values than these. Many of us can preach well enough, but *we* are wrong. We talk of the flesh but don't know its perils; we talk of the Spirit but would we recognize him were he really to move us? Too much of our work for God depends not on his will and purpose but on our feelings—or even, God forgive us! on the weather. Like chaff and stubble, it is carried away by the wind. Given the right mood we may accomplish a lot, but just as easily, in adverse conditions, we may down tools entirely. No, as the fire will one day prove, work that is dependent on feelings or on the wind of revival is of little use to God. When God commands, feelings or no feelings, we must learn to do.

Such values are costly. Those unwilling to pay the price will never come by them. Grace is free, but this isn't. Only a high price buys costly stones. Many a time we shall want to cry out "This is costing too much!" Yet the things wrought by God through the lessons we learn under his hand, though we be long in learning them—these are the really worthwhile things.

Time is an element in this. In the light of God, some things perish of themselves; there is no need to wait for the fire. It is in what remains, in what has stood God's test of time, that true worth lies. Here are found the precious stones, formed in what God graciously gives us of sorrow and trouble, as he puts us "through fire and water" to bring us to his wealthy place. Man sees the outward appearance; God sees the inward cost. Do not wonder that you experience all sorts of trials. Accepted from his hand they are the sure way to a life that is precious to him.

May God have mercy on the clever people, who give with one hand what they take with the other! Not even speaking for God can be done without cost. It is all a question whether the vessel is light or weighty, for weight shows the quality of the material. Two men may use the same words, but in the one you meet something you cannot get past; in the other—nothing. The difference is in the man. You always know when you are in the presence of spiritual worth. No amount of theorizing about the Lord's return, for example, will take the place of a life that has been daily lived looking for him. There is no escaping this difference, and no substitute for the real thing. Alas, some of us are so unlike our words that it might be better if we said less about spiritual things.

Do not wonder, then, at God's concern for the materials of his house. Imitation jewelry may have a certain beauty, but what woman that has once possessed the real thing would give it another thought? The apostle Paul leaves us in no doubt of his own valuation. Ten coolie-loads of stubble can never approach the price of one single gem. All flesh, all mere feelings, all that is essentially of man, is grass and must vanish away. What is of Christ, the gold, the silver, the costly stones, these alone are eternal, incorruptible, imperishable.

It is this lasting character of God's Church that must now claim our attention.

ETERNAL IN THE HEAVENS

It is in the later writings of the apostle Paul, and more especially in his Epistle to the Ephesians, that the eternal nature of the Church of Christ is given the greatest prominence. As the House, as the Body, as the Bride of Christ, as the people of God, the Church is a special theme of Ephesians. We have the Lord of the Body (Ch. 1), the material of the House (Ch. 2), the eternal mystery of the Church (Ch. 3), the growth of the Body (Ch. 4), the preciousness of the Bride (Ch. 5), and the warfare of the people of God (Ch. 6); and every one of these is seen in an eternal context. We have already touched on the third of these, and we now have to speak a little about Chapters 1, 2 and 5.

What is God doing today? Ephesians helps us to answer this question. First the apostle takes a backward look. "He chose us in him before the foundation of the world." "In him ... we were made a heritage, having been foreordained according to the purpose of him who worketh all things after the counsel of his will" (1:4, 11).

Here he shows us God working, not to a hoped-for end, but from a settled purpose. It is because God's eternal work first reaches back into the past that it then also reaches on into "the ages to come" (2:7).

Next the apostle looks forward. God has, he assures us, "made known unto us the mystery of his will, according to his good pleasure which he purposed in him unto a dispensation of the fullness of the times, to sum up all things in Christ" (1:9, 10). In this last clause he summarizes and defines God's work in time; it is "to sum up all things in Christ." To leave no loose ends of any kind, to have nothing out of harmony in his universe, to see realized in fullness in his own the oneness that now they only taste: that is his goal.

But instead, what is our common experience today? Perhaps a group of us are together in God's presence, and all that passes between us is so evidently of Christ, and therefore so good, that we feel we have touched the fullness. But then, at a point, one of us who should know better speaks or prays of himself—"after the flesh," as Paul would put it—and the life goes out of our fellowship. The spell is broken, and the thing we tasted has eluded us. Here on earth, how we long that such fellowship in Christ should be, in some measure at least, the normal experience in our churches and in our homes: "all one in Christ Jesus," with nothing that is outside of him! How we long and labor for this, and yet how hard it seems to realize it! We have to confess that to bring it to pass is impossible to us.

Yet we praise God that he calls us to have a share in this "impossible" work.

This is not a contradiction. God's fellow-laborer in this *is* the Church herself—every one of us, that is, and not merely preachers and special workers. And, praise God, Ephesians heartens us with the assurance that the oneness we but taste will indeed one day be true of the whole universe; there will be nothing outside of him.

In this letter Paul points us both back to paradise and forward to paradise, back to what God did before the creation (1:4) and on to what he is going to do to all generations (2:7), both of them in respect of the Church. God's Son himself is revealed in the Church, which is why she is here described as "his Body" (1:23). As a man's personality is expressed through his body, so is Christ displayed through the Church. She is in this age the vessel which, in a spiritual sense, contains and reveals Christ.

To be found "working together with God" does not mean that many men are called to "help" God. It means that what God has determined to do, the Church must make way for him to do in her. And if it is indeed God's purpose for ever to reveal his wisdom and power through her, then surely to miss this is to miss everything. Paul himself held that whatever else he did counted for nothing if he failed to apprehend that for which he was apprehended by Christ Jesus (Phil. 3:12). Ask yourself, "The work I have done, that for which I have lived and poured out my strength, what is it?" May God give us grace once again, if need be, to weigh out work in the balance of the sanctuary. We dare not live for a small thing. When, in the light of his Word, we see God's purpose in his Son, everything is transformed. We still preach, but we see differently. Nothing we do thereafter stands alone. All is for one thing—the eternal self-revelation of Christ through his Body.

A second wonderful thing that Ephesians discloses to us is this, that not only is the Church's work eternal; in the sight of God, it is also in heaven. The place of blessing where she is seated, her standing, life, ministry, warfare—everything is in "the heavens" and from "the heavens" (1:3, 20; 2:6; 3:10; 4:8-12; 6:12). This helps us to define further what it should mean to work for God. To create an earthly thing is easy for us. If we are content with an outward, technical Christianity—a "movement" based on an earthly foundation, with an earthly structure and organization—then it is quite possible to do the thing ourselves. But we have been apprehended for something utterly different from this. The Church is spiritual, and her work is heavenly. It must never become earthbound.

David "served his own generation," and slept (Acts 13:36). He could not serve two! Where today we seek to perpetuate our work by setting up an organization or society or system, the Old Testament saints served their own day and passed on. This is an important principle of life. Wheat is sown, grows, ears, is reaped, and then the whole plant, even to the root, is plowed out. That is the Church, never rooted permanently in the earth. God's work is the spiritual to the point of having no earthly roots, no smell of earth on it at all. Men pass on, but the Lord remains. The spiritual testimony of believers is to be heavenly, not earthly. Everything to do with the Church must be up-to-date and living, meeting the present—one could even say the passing—needs of the hour. Never must it become fixed, static. God himself takes away his workers, but he gives others. Our work suffers, but his never does. Nothing touches him. He is still God.

ONE NEW MAN

One very interesting consequence of this heavenly character of the Church appears in the second chapter, and in a parallel passage in Colossians. In Ephesians 2 Paul sets out to show how two mutually hostile elements in the world of his day, the Jews and the non-Jews, have been brought together by him to become one "holy temple in the Lord." What he has to say concerning this "habitation of God in the Spirit" is surprisingly different from what most Christians say today. Today it is widely held that, if the people of God of different race or background or Christian denomination are gathered on the agreed ground of a creed or "basis of faith," that is of the essence of the Church. To them, all sorts of Christians, of no matter what language or tradition or viewpoint or connection, *together* form the Church, and this is not affected by what various things they may carry in with them from outside.

The correction for this kind of thinking is the

word "new" in verse 15: "... that he might create in himself of the twain one new man." We think Jewish believers plus Gentile believers (or whatever other groupings are in our minds at the moment) are the Church. But to leave us in no doubt as to what the Holy Spirit means, Paul expresses the same thing even more explicitly in Colossians 3:11. Writing once again of the new man, he says that within its sphere: "there cannot be Greek and Jew, circumcision and uncircumcision, barbarian, Scythian, bondman, freeman: but Christ is all, and in all." If we understand him aright this means that, if we want to be Christians, we cannot be anything else *but* Christians!

The trouble is that much of our thinking about these things starts from a false premise. Let me try to illustrate. Imagine yourself standing outside the door of the Church, symbolically giving away bread to the hungry. Any who care to do so are free to come and take a little, regardless of what they may be engaged in or encumbered with. All sorts and conditions of men come, and they eat. Are they not qualified to enter? And will they live together peaceably if they do? Your first reaction may be to answer yes, regarding the rabble that have gathered as partaking of a fellowship that unifies them on the basis of what they have received. But wait a minute! What about the bulky articles in their hands, and the burdens on their shoulders? What about the animals they drive before them, and the cartloads of furniture and merchandise they drag behind? You are overlooking what comes in with them when they come in. They have with them all the makings of a busy market, or worse!

Look again. The door is narrow. A Cross overshadows it, and beyond it lies a tomb. If the bread you distribute spoke of a shared life, these symbolize something else. They tell us that in entering, not only is there something to be received; there is something also to be relinquished. "Having abolished in his flesh the enmity" he made both one (Eph. 2:15). There was in fallen man something to be broken down that constituted a positive barrier to fellowship, and that had to go.

We cannot evade this other symbol. We cannot escape this second condition of fellowship in life. Whatever our nationality or color or Christian denomination, we must die, for only those who have been crucified with Christ, only those who have let go of something, find themselves at home there. Natural traits, national rivalries, class traditions, personal preferences, all the things that we would instinctively clutch to ourselves and seek to carry over, as it were, from the old life and order—all are by the Cross excluded. God's "new man" is altogether and only new. Inside those limits, what is of Christ alone is found, and he must be "all and in all."

FROM THE BEGINNING

From what we have already said it will be evident that Ephesians sets out to give us the highest New Testament revelation of the Church. This appears again in the order in which the

Church's history is treated in this letter. Here, as we have suggested, we not only see her as from sin redeemed; we are shown too her course from the beginning of creation. Whereas Romans introduces sin in Chapter 1, and only approaches the subject of the Body of Christ in Chapter 12 after dealing at length with the justification and sanctification of the individual sinner, Ephesians begins differently, going back further into history to do so. It is striking that, as early as Ephesians 1, the Church comes into view as already "chosen in Christ," and that even though the question of sin follows hard after this statement, it is not treated at any length until Chapter 2. The letter as a whole sets out, in fact, to give us the Church's complete history, comprising both her place in the fullness of God's purpose in Christ and the work of God's grace by which he redeemed her to bring her there.

This view of the Church goes back to the very start of things. It sees her there in the mind of God much as Eve appears in the second chapter of Genesis, before the irruption of sin into the creation.[1] This comparison makes Eve unusual, even unique, among the women of the Old Testament who may be felt to be types of the Church. In each of them some aspect of the Church is depicted. We see her presented to the bridegroom (Rebekah), chosen from among the Gentiles (Asenath), passing through the wilderness (Zipporah), receiving her inheritance in the

---

[1]While the Church was no doubt revealed to man only long after the Fall, we must, I think, allow that she was planned by God before it.

land (Achsah), altogether dependent upon her kinsman-redeemer (Ruth), and militant for her Lord (Abigail). Yet, interesting as is this sequence of types, none is so instructive as that presented by Eve. For they all succeed the Fall, and therefore directly or indirectly have moral issues and responsibilities associated with them. But Eve, viewed as in that blessed period before sin entered, remains uniquely typical of the Church as the one who fulfills all God's desire for her in union with his Son.

For Eve was one and alone; and she was absolutely for Adam. "Have ye not read," said Jesus, "that he which made them from the beginning made them male and female, and said, For this cause shall a man leave his father and mother, and shall cleave to his wife; and the twain shall become one flesh?" (Matt. 19:4, 5). At this point the spiritual type, preceding the entry of sin and for the present untouched by it, expresses most perfectly God's original and eternal intention to have a Bride for his Son.

Moreover the figure of the Church that Eve presents is a double figure, and this may help us to understand Paul's language in Ephesians. First, as a part of Adam, taken from him in sleep, she was his body. Then, created, perfected and brought again to him, she became his bride. Other created things were brought to him, but not being *of* him they could not be his helpmeet. This distinguishes Eve from the rest of the creation. It also typically distinguishes the Church of Christ from the entire old creation today.

For sin *has* entered. The Fall is a fact of history. "Through one man's disobedience the many were made sinners." "The whole creation groaneth and travaileth in pain together until now." The work of redemption thus became a divine necessity. The Cross had to become history, not merely now to fulfill the figure of sleep and waking and new creation foreshadowed by the sleep of Adam. It must deal as well with the new situation the Fall has created.[2] Sin and death must by it be met and done away. Christ Jesus must humble himself for our sakes, becoming obedient even to the death of the cross. The price must be paid and Satan's power broken. Every individual sinner must come to the Savior and find remission of sins through the atoning blood. So it is that we see ourselves—and rightly—as in the valley of sin, the trophies of redemption. That, as I said, is Romans. Yet even after all this history, Ephesians finds God choosing, rather, to view us as within his eternal purpose, altogether *from* Christ and altogether *for* Christ.

Here is the miracle of divine hope, that even the disaster of the Fall could not frustrate but could only hinder. Adam has sinned; and apart from the grace of God, man in the flesh—yes, even redeemed man—can, and would repeatedly, sin. But by new birth there is planted in him that of Christ which sin cannot touch, and he is commanded to live by that. The very life of

[2]This is perhaps the reason why, unlike that of believers, the death of Jesus is never described in the New Testament merely in terms of "sleep."

Christ himself, released by the Cross and distributed to his members, supplies them with the power to do so. By it, sin's dominion over them is broken; in its resurrection newness, they walk (Rom. 6:4, 6). There is no substitute. It alone can meet God's demands.

And it is to be shared, for in the sphere of divine purpose there are not many individual vessels, but one Vessel. God created one Eve, not many men. Without Christ, I personally do not possess life; without the Church his Body, I have not the means to live the life I possess as it should be lived.

But now, not only do I have the life; I have also with me the Giver of life himself. Let us return for a moment to the latter part of Ephesians 5. In the passage from verses 25-30 I think we can distinguish these two things, the Bride and the Body. In verses 25-27 we have the first law of love, "Husbands, love your wives," and it is based upon two things: the past tense of Christ's love for his Bride, expressed in his death on her behalf, and the future tense of his purpose for her. This is the *eternal* view. Again in verses 28-30 we have a second law of love, "Husbands ought also to love their own wives as their own bodies," and this is based upon one thing: the present tense of Christ's love for that which is, in essence, himself, his Body. This latter is the view *today*. The first passage sees Christ and his Church apart, having separate existence, and is concerned with her union, as Bride, with him, the Giver of life. The second sees Christ and his Church spiritually identified, without separate existence, and concerns her identification and present unity of life with him as his Body. From One there have become two; from being two they will again be one. This is the mystery of the Church, that all that is from Christ returns to him.

The work of Christ now is to love and cherish her, to protect and preserve her from disease and blemish, caring thus for her because he loves her as his own self—because, speaking reverently, the Church *is* Christ! How does he nourish and preserve her? "By the washing of water with the word" (verse 26). In this verse "the word" is not *Logos*, the great, objective, eternal Word of God; it is *rhema*, the smaller, more personal and subjective spoken word. "The words *(rhemata)* that I have spoken unto you are spirit, and are life" (John 6:63). *Rhema* always suggests to us something very personal and intimate: "Mary said, Behold the handmaid of the Lord; be it unto me according to thy word." "Now lettest thou thy servant depart, O Lord, according to thy word, in peace." "The word of God came unto John the son of Zacharias in the wilderness." "We toiled all night, and took nothing: but at thy word I will let down the nets." "He is not here, but is risen: remember how he spake unto you when he was yet in Galilee.... And they remembered his words." "The Holy Ghost fell on them.... And I remembered the word of the Lord, how that he said, ... Ye shall be baptized with the Holy Ghost." (Luke 1:38; 2:29; 3:2; 5:5; 24:6-8; Acts 11:15, 16.)

How is the Church's return to the plan of God

effected? "By water *with* the word": the water of his risen life, checking us and exposing, by contrast with itself, all that needs to be eliminated; and his word, dealing with what has been revealed, and renewing us by cleansing away the blemishes. Sometimes maybe the word comes first and then the life, but the effect is the same. "The second time the cock crew. And Peter called to mind the word ... And when he thought thereon, he wept" (Mark 14:72). The Church to which God's word has no power to appeal is no Church. But the word is his instrument of cleansing and renewal. If only we realize this, and allow it to do its work, though we may fail, we shall not long remain unaware that we have done so.

And blessed be God, the day will come when the Body, taking its character wholly from him who is its life, will have been made ready to become the Bride, his helpmeet. Because, as his Body, she has attained to the measure of the stature of his fullness (4:13) she will be presented to him at the last, "a glorious Church, not having spot or wrinkle or any such thing" (5:27). Wholly like him because wholly of him, she will be wholly for him. She has expressed his glory; she will be presented to him clothed in that glory, with no scar of sin, no wrinkle of age, no time wasted, no flaw of any kind, but holy and without blemish. Christ, by his word, has left in her no ground for Satan or demons, men or angels—no, nor yet even for God himself—to lay any charge against her. For in her, now, all is new, and all is of God. Should we not, then, if this is to be its blessed effect, greatly treasure the word that God speaks to us today?

7
Building in Love

From the heavenly mystery we turn now to the earthly expression. Having seen the Church, the Body, in her relation to her Lord, we must now consider her human relationships. The time has come to ask ourselves, How do the members function one towards another?

It seems likely that, of all the apostles, it was to Paul first that there came the concept of Jesus and his people as a body and its members. Certainly it is a view of the Church that is peculiarly his. It was, after all, bound up with his very conversion and calling, being contained in the Lord's first words to him: "I am Jesus whom thou persecutest" (Acts 9:5). To persecute those who believe is to persecute Jesus. To touch his disciples is to touch him. Thus these words heralded the great revelation that was to be given to Paul of the mystery of the Church. They told him something new about the Lord, something till then no more than implicit in his statements while on earth.

But the Lord did not leave the matter there with Paul. He did not allow him to stay with the heavenly mystery. The command that immediately followed came right down to the practical consequences of such a revelation. "Rise, and enter into the city, and it shall be told thee what thou must do." *It shall be told thee.* Apart from those very disciples against whom he had set himself, Paul would be helpless; he would never know. The Lord himself would not tell him what to do, save on the basis of the living Church. He would not lend his support to a merely individual calling and mission. For individualism is sin; it does injury to the Body of Christ.

So Paul reached Damascus, and there followed for him long hours of waiting. At first no man came. Only after three days of darkness did someone at length arrive—and even then, he was but "a disciple." From Luke's use of this simple title we are to conclude that Ananias, though devout and of honorable character, was just an ordinary brother, with nothing special about him to qualify him as the helper of the destined "great apostle of the Church." But it is just here that the mystery of the Church must become practical for Paul.

And for his part too, Ananias, who knew Saul of Tarsus by repute and had every reason to fear him, must now give practical expression to a miracle of divine grace in his own heart. His cautious "this man" (Acts 9:13) becomes "Brother Saul" (verse 17). Jesus has slain the enmity and all his fears are dispelled. Ananias's simple words of greeting express, in brother-to-brother terms, the recognition by the universal Church of another member of Christ, while his simple act demonstrated the newfound oneness of these two men under a single anointing. In one Spirit they gave and received instructions that were designed by God to have a worldwide outcome (Acts 22:14-16).

In his writings Paul gives us two somewhat different views of the Body, one in Ephesians and the other in 1 Corinthians. Whereas the one sees the Church in the heavenlies, the other sees her planted firmly on the earth. In Ephesians the Church—*all* of it—is the Body. To the Corinthian believers Paul can nevertheless write: "Ye are the body of Christ, and severally members thereof" (1 Cor. 12:27). If, as many do, we regard Ephesians as a circular letter, this may help to explain why Paul, thinking in large, universal terms, occupies himself there with *the* Body of Christ, whereas in 1 Corinthians, writing this time to the church in a particular Greek city, he shows us that Body functioning in a given situation on the earth, and doing so in the way *a* body functions.

That, I take it, is the explanation of a significant little clause in 1 Corinthians 12:21: "The eye cannot say to the hand, I have no need of thee: or again the head to the feet, I have no need of you." We should be careful not to misunderstand Paul here. The Body of Christ, whether universally in heaven or locally on earth, has only one Head, Christ himself (Eph. 4:15). There cannot be many local "heads" of churches, or there would at once be schism in the Body, and Paul is not suggesting that there can. Rather is he using in 1 Corinthians the *metaphor* of a human body to illustrate practical principles of relatedness and function, by which the heavenly and eternal Body of Christ operates *down here*. Just as the Head, Christ, cannot dispense with the least of his members, so, he affirms, can no single member get along without any other member.

Thus in First Corinthians we see the whole matter treated in relation not so much to divine purpose as to human responsibility. The former is essential, for none could function without it, but the question is, are we bringing it down and applying it where we are today?

The problem seems to be to have the two. It is easy to accept the Ephesian side—the heavenly view of what God will have. Our troubles begin with 1 Corinthians. For the spiritually minded that letter is altogether too practical, and because it is so, they are always in danger of evading the difficulties of its application. They seek (and rightly) to avoid the extreme of deducing, from the available evidence of New Testament practices, a foolproof pattern or system of church life and then following that slavishly. They know only too well this will produce but a lifeless copy of that historic beginning. So instead they fix their eyes almost exclusively upon the glorious heavenly Church set forth in Ephesians, only to fall into the opposite error—that of keeping the vision so "spiritual" that it becomes almost, if not quite, imaginary!

Yet 1 Corinthians 12 is a very simple passage, and perhaps it is just because it is so simple that its meaning is missed by many. What is here is not heavenly, nor is it earthly, *but heavenly and yet expressed on earth*. The revelation of the Body in the heavenlies is intended spontaneously to issue in very practical results, and it is these results that are there defined.

God's principle is the principle of incarnation.[1] God desires—indeed for him it is more than a desire; it is a divine necessity—to show the heavenly life in an earth expression, not in angels or spirits but in men, not as something vague and imaginary but in a form that is real and practical. It is blessed to be living in the heavenlies in Ephesians, but remember, the same apostle who wrote Ephesians also wrote Corinthians. God's character demands that his Church, universal, spiritual, heavenly, should have its earthly expression in local churches, set in places no less dark than the pagan city of Corinth. And because there is this earthly expression, men will always be ready enough to

[1]We use the term with caution. It is unwise to carry too far the parallel between the Church and her incarnate Lord.

step in with their opinions, and have a hand in the arrangements. "We must be earthly *sometimes!*" they say in extenuation. But 1 Corinthians 12 shows us that, even in such an earthly environment, the church is still to operate on the principles of the heavenly Body. For the local church is not merely an outward type, it is a real manifestation of Christ in the earth today. "Ye are the Body of Christ." Here in Corinth you Corinthian believers are called to be the whole Body in essence.

TAKING RESPONSIBILITY

So we turn to 1 Corinthians 12 and its treatment of the functional life of the Body. If we look closely at the section of this chapter from verse 12 onwards, I think we can discern four simple laws governing the Body's life.

The first is in verses 15 and 16: "If the foot shall say, Because I am not the hand, I am not of the body; it is not therefore not of the body. And if the ear shall say, Because I am not the eye, I am not of the body; it is not therefore not of the body." In other words, you must function as you are, and not as you would prefer to be. Because you are not someone else, that is no ground for declining to be yourself! It is as though the foot said, "I had made up my mind to be a hand, and because I can't, I'll refuse to walk!" Such refusal springs from a comparing heart, and only individualism compares.

This habit of making comparisons reveals one thing, that we have not yet seen the Body of

Christ. For tell me, which is the better member, the foot or the hand? There is, when you come to think of it, no way of comparing them. Their function in the human body is different, and each is equally needed there. And yet many thus minimize God's gift. Because they cannot be the special member they admire, they decline to take their place at all. Or they think all ministry begins and ends with public ministry, and because they have not the gift to function in a public way, they do nothing.

That is exactly the situation described in Jesus' parable of the men with the talents (Matthew 25:14-30). There was a servant with five talents and another with two, but the whole emphasis in the parable is on the one-talent man. The danger is of the one-talent brother burying his talent. "Since I have not got five talents, or two, what can I possibly do with one? Since I cannot minister in a conspicuous way, am I really any use at all? Since others are so well able to lead in prayer and set the tone of the prayer-meeting, is it not all right for me to keep silent? I cannot occupy a place of prominence; does it matter therefore whether I occupy any place at all?"

But the parable teaches that if two can grow into four, and five into ten, one can grow into two. It is by functioning that we discover life. The Church is suffering not as much from the prominence of the five-talent members as from the holding back of the one-talent members. The life of the whole Body is hampered and impoverished by the burial of those single talents.

If we have once recognized the heavenly Body,

we shall be very glad to have the tiniest part in it. Of course, refusal to function because we have only one talent may reveal in us desires and ambitions outside the will of God, or worse, a dissatisfaction with that will. But no, if it pleases him to make me the greatest member, praise the Lord! If he chooses instead to make me the least, praise him no less! Am I a hand, or a foot? I will gladly be just that. I am perfectly satisfied with his choice, and willing to function in his appointed sphere, and if I accept his gift and use it, the one can grow to two, and very quickly there will be five or even ten.

Paul wrote: "Encourage the fainthearted" (1 Thess. 5:14), and the word is literally "small-souled." We should encourage the one-talent man, not because of the magnitude of his gift—it isn't so very big after all—but because the Holy Spirit indwells him. His ground of expectation is to be God himself. One of my own closest colleagues, before he was born again, was regarded by his friends as incredibly dull, indeed almost stupid. Yet when God took hold of his life and the Holy Spirit began to work in him, within two years he already showed signs of becoming, as he now is, one of the most gifted Bible teachers in China.

So the first law of function is that we use what we have been given. We cannot excuse ourselves and say, "I am not needed here." Nor shall we find spiritual refreshment by taking our Bibles and notebooks and retiring to a quiet spot to prepare for some imagined future ministry, if in so doing we are evading a present responsibility.

Our physical body may be refreshed thereby, but not our spirit. No, the rule is always to serve others with what we have in hand, and as we do so, to discover that we ourselves are fed. Recall the story of Jesus at the well. He was hungry, for he had sent his disciples to buy food, and thirsty, for he asked the Samaritan woman for a drink. But when the disciples came back he could claim to have eaten. He had been strengthened by doing the will of God in ministering to one soul in need.

The fellowship of the Body is always two-way; receiving and giving. Wanting only to receive is not fellowship. We may not be preachers, but when we come to worship we nevertheless bring what we have. There must be help of the pulpit from the pew. Sitting and looking on will not do. We must give others to drink, not necessarily by speaking, but maybe by quiet prayer. And if we do just sit and listen, we must *be there* in spirit, not somewhere else!

"Occupy till I come": what a great range of ministry we have got *where we are!* The bit of work entrusted to us is for the Body, so there is no room for jealousy of others. We cannot draw comparisons, and complain to our brother, "God uses you and he doesn't use me." Would some of us prefer to be like Peter and win souls? Let us remember, the eleven stood up with Peter. Peter was the mouthpiece, but he could never dare to say, "I won those souls."

So every member of the Body has a ministry, and every member is called to function in the place appointed by the Lord. It makes no difference who does the work if the glory is his. We must turn to God's account the position given us by him, and not run off hoping to grow in retirement. "I was afraid, and went away and hid thy talent in the earth." There can be no glory in that direction.

ACCEPTING LIMITATION

The second law of function is found in verses 17 and 18: "If the whole body were an eye, where were the hearing? If the whole were hearing, where were the smelling? But now hath God set the members each one of them in the body, even as it pleased him." The principle here set forth is that, in our life together, we are always to leave room for the function of others.

Putting it bluntly, do not try to do everything and be everything yourself! No one in his senses would desire to see the whole Body function merely in a single way. It is not reasonable for the whole to be an eye, nor for the eye to attempt the work of the whole. The Lord has ordered variety in the Body, an ear and a nose as well as an eye and a hand; not conformity, and certainly not single-organ monopoly. Thus, if the previous principle was for those lagging behind, this one is for those who are too forward, wanting to be the whole Body. The word to them is, I repeat, Don't try to do or be everything; you are not everything!

There are those who, when they come to a prayer meeting, can only pray themselves; they cannot listen to others. They are willing to lead but not to be led in prayer. They want others to listen and say "Amen," but they are too impatient to listen and say "Amen" to what another prays. They want their own contribution to be the high light of the meeting. They are individualists, even when in prayer with others.

In conversation too they are individualists. They can only talk about themselves and their work. They cannot listen while the work of others is spoken of without breaking in with something about themselves. They lack the ability to receive. Individualism is a distressing feature of Christian work. It means that *our* work, *our* ministry, becomes so important that we have no interest in what others are doing.

There is much frustration and loss among the members of Christ today because some of us who are experienced servants of God are not willing to let others function. We have been given a ministry by the Lord, and for this reason we think we must bear the whole responsibility ourselves if others are to develop and grow. We have not understood that by doing so we are in fact hindering the development of those others. This mistake is a fruitful source of discouragement and even division, and its ill effects do not end there.

For let us suppose that I encounter a doctrinal point of which I cannot see the answer, and find myself in a fog about it. What do I do? Do I try to decide it myself, or do I go to the member whose special gift from God is the capacity to teach and clarify, and to lead people out of doctrinal fogs? If I do the former, I have opened the way for a new doctrinal difference, for it is at this very point that doctrinal differences have their birth. Instead of trusting the Lord to solve my problem through his teaching member, and so letting another member function for me in this matter, I have made it all too possible for the two of us to be found teaching different and even conflicting things. If, for example, as an evangelist, I take on also the teaching of my converts, this kind of confusion is very liable to occur. Rather must I serve, and then when my function is fulfilled, stand aside and make room for another. For a first principle of the Body is that "he that planteth and he that watereth are one" (1 Cor. 3:8).

As a member, I must be prepared to receive what another member has to give. For myself I must be willing for limitation. Is the church at prayer? I must be ready to remain silent and to give room for the "weaker" prayers. Have I a gift of preaching? I must learn to sit and listen to others. Be my measure small or large, I dare not, as a member, go beyond it, for the mark of the Cross is upon all that is oversize, all that is extraneous to the Body. I must be willing to be limited entirely to my sphere, and to let others serve in theirs. I must be happy for others to function towards me, and to accept the help ministered to me by them.

ESTEEMING OTHERS

Third, we come to verses 21 and 22: "The eye cannot say to the hand, I have no need of thee: or

again the head to the feet, I have no need of you.
Nay, much rather, those members of the body
which seem to be more feeble are necessary." Put
quite simply, we must never seek to cut off another member. We must not think we can act in
the capacity of the Head and dispense with the
members. Weakness or uncouthness in a
member is no warrant for our cutting him off.[2]
We dare not say to another: "I have no need of
thee." Rather do we discover how much we can
learn from members we would not naturally es-
teem. We may often have to call for prayer help
from those we might even be inclined to despise.
Alas, how readily do we feel we should demean
ourselves and lose our spiritual status by so doing! Yet the Lord affirms that he has a place for,
and can use, even the feeblest of his members.

Once, years ago, I was facing a very big problem in my life. It concerned the whole question
of personal enduement with the Holy Spirit for
service. I was both under a deep sense of the
need for this, and also in some confusion of
mind about the doctrine. Yet somehow, pray as I
might, the Lord seemed unwilling either to answer my questions or to show me the way
through into the experience. I knew he had
something more for me, but it remained out of
my reach, and I felt I must somehow get clear on
this or I could not go on. It is no exaggeration to
say that my whole ministry hung in the balance.

I was engaged at the time in preaching the

[2]Of course there is such a thing as discipline in the Church
where sin is concerned. Of this we shall speak later, but this
is not what is in view here.

gospel in a remote part of the country, far removed from other servants of God with anything approaching the knowledge of the Lord that I felt I had. I had been sent there by him, and there was no doubt of the need or of the readiness of people to hear. But something was lacking. My preaching was void of power, and there was very little fruit from it. Yet what God was seeking to give me I seemed unable to receive. I could not get through alone; what I needed above all just then was fellowship.

But where was I to find it? True there was a handful of simple believers, country folk, among whom I had been staying, but I felt they knew so little of the Lord that they certainly could not help me in the great problem facing me. They would scarcely even have a sufficient foundation from which to pray intelligently for me in it, and certainly not enough to bring me through. I was forgetting the Body!

At last I reached an impasse. There was nothing left but to call them in, if I was not to give up and go out altogether. So at my request those simple brethren came to me in my need. I told them what I could of my difficulty, and they prayed—and as they prayed, light dawned! The thing did not *need* explaining. It was done, and done in such a way that it has never needed to be repeated. From that day on the tide of blessing flowed.

Yes, God will bring us often to places where we cannot get through alone. For the life that asserts that "God and I are enough" is only in fact hindering him. The Lord taught me that day how those members of the Body which seem to be more feeble are indeed to him most precious.

KEEPING THE UNITY

And fourth, verses 24 and 25 tell us: "God tempered the body together, giving more abundant honor to that part which lacked; that there should be no schism in the body; but that the members should have the same care one for another." What the apostle here says in conclusion is that we are resolutely to refuse schism. It is totally disallowed. The divine will is that *there should be no schism in the Body.*

In previous chapters we have spoken of unity in general terms. The Church, as seen in heaven, cannot be divided. Praise God, it is one for ever. Yes, but there can be inroads upon that unity in the church on earth. As to its heavenly life the Body is untouchable; but in its functioning on earth it is all too sadly true that it can be touched and even mutilated, as the Corinthian situation abundantly shows. Paul condemns this state of affairs in no uncertain terms.

What, then, is the secret of practical unity? Here are two statements about it. "For in one Spirit were we all baptized into one body, whether Jews or Greeks, whether bond or free; and were all made to drink of one Spirit" (1 Cor. 12:13). "There is one body and one Spirit" (Eph. 4:4). What they reveal is a remarkable relation between the Body and the Spirit. The hidden reality, the Spirit, has its counterpart in the manifestation, the Body. The Body is one because the Spirit is one. For remember, the Holy Spirit is a Person and you cannot subdivide a person. "God tempered the body together," because the one Body is to be a manifestation of the one Spirit. There is always unity in the Spirit. The divine fact is certain. The only question is, do we always give diligence to keep the unity? (Eph. 4:3).

Before proceeding to a further word about the Holy Spirit and the Body, let us remind ourselves that the starting-point for spiritual unity is life. You may already have observed that the four principles we have outlined above are not in fact expressed as command at all. They appear in 1 Corinthians 12 in the form of statements of what the Body *is like*. They describe it in terms of the spontaneous manifestations of life and growth in a human body. This is significant, and it brings us to consider an important feature of life, namely, consciousness.

All animal life has its consciousness, but especially is this true of life from God. Where there is life there is consciousness. A biologist has no way of taking up life as a separate thing and handing it to us to touch or look at, nor is there any way by which we could see it if he did. Yet all will agree that, because of our inward consciousness, we know we have life. We are in no doubt at all that we live.

And the same is true of the new life. Though the life that God gives cannot be handled or seen, it is certainly possible for us to be conscious of it. We know new life because with it there is awakened in us a new consciousness. When a man is born again, he receives new life from God. How does he *know* he has received it? How do any of us know we possess new life? We know by a new life-consciousness. If the life is there, the consciousness will be there and will very soon manifest itself, towards God, and towards sin. If we sin there is distress. We lose something of our peace and joy. It is this that proves the presence of life. Because the life of God hates sin, there has come to be in us a new consciousness towards sin. When a man constantly needs someone to point out his sins to him and is otherwise unaware of them himself, then, however willing to listen he may be, it is more than doubtful whether he possesses life.

Today we place great emphasis on life, but that is not enough. We should emphasize also the consciousness of life. A being without consciousness has very little evidence of life. For it is a misunderstanding to think of life as abstract. It is concrete, real. In a human heart, either new life is present or it is absent, and life-consciousness is what confirms its presence. Nor is this consciousness merely negative, towards sin. It is also blessedly positive, towards God himself. The Spirit witnesses with our spirit that we are the children of God—yes, but it is no use *telling* people that! Either they know it, or they don't. If they possess God's life they know it by the Spirit. Many, sad to say, pray prayers which have neither consciousness of sin nor love to God in them. One can only describe them as angels' prayers, for they bear none of the marks of the prayers of God's children.

But if what we have said is true of the life of the individual, it is no less true of the life of the Body. Those who possess life possess it in common with others, and they who know the Body are conscious of the corporate character of that life. For the Body is not only a principle or a doctrine; it too, implies a consciousness. As we are conscious of new life, so, if we are within the Body, we must necessarily be conscious also of that.

Some act towards the Body much as people do who determine to love their enemies because it is a Christian duty, or not to tell lies because it is wrong. But while it is very important whether we lie or not, what is far more important is whether, if we do, we are troubled inside. Inner consciousness of God and inner sensitiveness to sin are the basis of Christianity, these and not outward rules. So it is little use trying to live by the principle of the Body unless we are conscious that something is wrong when we do not. It is one thing to be told, and quite another to see. Consciousness is that inner sense that sees *without* being told. If the entrance of divine light can give in our hearts the consciousness of God, and of sin that is against God, it can give a like consciousness of the Body, and of conduct that is against Christ as Head of the Body. It was light from God that awakened in Paul a consciousness of the Body, and showed him that he was opposing himself to Jesus in the person of his members. Without the consciousness that comes from revelation and life, all is empty indeed.

"LOVE ONE ANOTHER"

Let me try now to illustrate the working of this faculty that I have called "Body-consciousness"—this sensitiveness to the Body of Christ. It works first of all in the matter of love. "We know that we have passed out of death into life, because we love the brethren" (1 John 3:14). All, who are members of the Body, love. This is remarkable. It is not that any need to wait till they are told. Spontaneously, whether they think about it or not, they love. They may need exhortation, but that is in order to stir up what they have. I remember a friend telling me how, when his first child was put into his arms, his heart went out in love to him. No one needed to tell him it was a father's duty to love his child. He simply found love there. But is it not equally true that, no matter who or what a brother is, as soon as you know he is a Christian, your heart goes out in love to him? This is consciousness of the Body.

It works also in regard to division. Whereas in respect of love it is active and positive, in respect of division it is passive and negative. To those who have truly discovered the meaning of the Body, all division, and everything that makes for division is hateful in the extreme. To be found differentiating between Christians is, for them, to have stepped into a foreign world. Whether it is right or not to glory in denominationalism, those who recognize the Body of Christ know that to do so is an impossibility. A sectarian spirit, however hallowed by tradition and use, soon becomes intolerable to the man who possesses life.

Again, factions and cliques are becoming far too common among Christians today. There may be a company of twenty believers, all born of the Spirit, gathering around the Lord. In comes a brother, and immediately draws to himself a separate clique of a few. That is not the Body, and it cannot become the Body. But if, knowing our oneness in him, we find ourselves drawn into doing such things, do we not at once become inwardly conscious of wrong? Something is surely lacking if we do not. If the Body means anything to us, all that divides, within and without, becomes abhorrent. Even to begin to create division is to forfeit our inward peace. We know we cannot go on. The consciousness of the one life will not allow it, and that is the sufficient answer.

This is not doctrine, but the living consciousness of our fellowship in Christ, and it is a very precious thing. The instant life comes to us, it awakens in us a growing and deepening sense of "belonging." We can no longer live a self-interested, self-sufficient Christian life. The nature of the butterfly, always "going it alone," has given place in us to the nature of the bee, always operating from the hive, always working not for itself but for the whole. Body-consciousness means that we see our own standing before God, not as isolated units but as members one of another.

Units have no special use, exercise no ministry, can easily be overlooked or left out. Whether they are present or not is no one's concern. They scarcely affect even statistics. But members are otherwise. They cannot be passive in the Body; they dare not merely stand by looking on. For none are so hurtful as onlookers. Whether or not we take a public part in things is immaterial; we must always be giving life, so that our absence is felt. We cannot say, "I don't count." We dare not attend meetings merely as passengers, while others do the work. We are his Body, and members in particular, and it is when all the members fulfill their ministry that the life flows.

For all is bound up with life and the source of life. The head is the life-source of the human body; injure it, and all movement, all coordination ceases. A headless torso has neither life nor consciousness of life. As members of Christ, we receive new life from him; but that life is "in the Son"; it is not something that we can carry away with us apart from him. Detach us for one moment from Christ, and we should have no life. We well know how even a shadow between ourselves and him may stem for a while its flow. For our life is *in him;* we possess nothing in ourselves. They have the life who have the Son.

God does not therefore tell us to hold fast our fellow members, but to "hold fast the Head." This is the way of fellowship. For Christ is not divided; he is one. Lay hold of him, and we shall find welling up in our heart a spontaneous love for all who do the same.

Oneness is Christ's, not ours. Because we are his, *therefore* we are one. For example, to say we have fellowship with a brother because we like him is to violate the oneness by centering it in ourselves. Though we may not naturally take to some so readily as to others, to let this affect our fellowship is simply to reveal its false basis. Or again, do we do something for a brother, and then complain of his ingratitude? That can only be because we did it seeking thanks, and not for Christ's sake—not because, in the first place, God so loved us. Our motive was wrong, because our relation to the Head was deficient.

It is "holding fast" to our fellow members that leads to exclusive friendships. The Body has no room for these. If one Christian becomes infatuated with another, so that an unhealthy friendship develops, sure enough, before long their friendship will issue in faction. For fellowship that is "after the flesh" is on a wrong foundation and can only lead eventually to sorrow. When two members cling exclusively to one another, we may justifiably fear that the love they express is not purely of God. "Love one another" is either something in the sphere of the Body, and therefore Christ-centered, or it is wrong. May God save us from uncrucified natural choices, and help us in these things to follow the Spirit.

The anointing of the Spirit is God's gift to every babe in Christ (1 John 2:18-20, 27). When we received Christ as Head we received the anointing—indeed the absence of it would be serious evidence that we were not yet united to him (Rom. 8:9). John shows us this anointing as an inward thing, conveying even to those babes in Christ the teaching of the Spirit "concerning

all things"—that is, not just concerning the
Scriptures. What do I mean? Let us take a practical illustration. Suppose I want to know whether
or not to make a trip to Hong Kong. How do I
decide? Do I seek a verse of Scripture? Or the
advice of friends? Or do I set my mind to decid-
ing the right or wrong of it? No, as we have often
said, the basis of our life is not "good or bad" but
the anointing. "Is the Holy Spirit in this thing? Is
my heart empty or full as I approach it?" It is not
a question of feeling or comparison, but of an
enquiry Godward: "Goes the Spirit witness life?
Does he assure me of the Father's good pleasure
in this step?" That is the only safe test. For while
the way we choose may be perfectly correct in
itself, what really matters is that the Spirit is
moving that way.

Herein lies the simplicity of the life of God's
children. There is no need for so much questioning. Disobedience to the anointing will very
soon give us a bad time with the Lord, whereas
the mind of the Spirit is always life and peace
(Rom. 8:6).

Because the Spirit is one, when his children
move thus, there will be no problems about fellowship. For the Body knows one law: that of the
anointing. Rules are good in society, but not in
the Body. The Pharisees were fundamentalists as
far as the letter of the Old Testament was concerned. They lived by the letter; they knew all
the rules—and so, perhaps we might feel, do we.
But what if our knowledge of those rules permits
us, as it did Saul of Tarsus, to stifle the Holy
Spirit's voice? He knew the law, it is true, but he

knew nothing of the Son of man in heaven (Acts 7:55, 56). And to quench the Spirit is to stifle the very consciousness of our life together as the heavenly Man. It is to injure our relationship to the Head just as terribly as an affection of the nerves of a limb severs that limb from effective control by the higher centers. Do this, and soon, like Saul, we shall be found breathing out threatening and slaughter.

Saul's life of fellowship began when he said, "What shall I do, Lord?" That is the secret. To "hold fast the Head" is to *obey* Christ through the Spirit. To follow the Spirit is to be subject to the Lord Jesus in all things. The Spirit will never never impose that obedience on the members, but they who live by the anointing will always, instinctively and gladly, subject themselves to Christ; and in doing so, they will discover their oneness. Oh, to see him, then, as unquestioned Lord!

8
Ministering Life

The highest purpose of God for the Church today is that she should build herself up in love by a ministry of life, and so grow up in all things into Christ. This is the goal set before her in Ephesians 4. Moreover in 1 Corinthians 13, a chapter that follows immediately on the passage about the Body we have just been considering, Paul shows us that it is love, not gifts, that God uses for the lasting edification of the Church. Gifts are expressed outwardly in works and speech, by miracles, healings, prophecy and so forth. Love is the fruit of the Holy Spirit's inward working through the Cross in the lives of the members. Gifts are the temporary method—God's method, to be sure—but it is in love that the Body builds itself up (Eph. 4:16). And when all else passes away, love remains.

Here we have an example of something we shall now take account of as we come to consider the ministry of the Church. I refer to the frequent emphasis in Paul's writings upon the better of two good things. Sometimes, within a given context, that emphasis is quite strong; at other times it is only implicit, but none the less to be taken account of. In this instance he is laying stress on permanency. Notwithstanding much that is said elsewhere about spiritual gifts, when in 1 Corinthians he contrasts them with love, he draws attention to their comparative impermanence (verses 8-11).

Spiritual gifts may not necessarily, in a given instance, be intended by God to be lasting; for gifts need not be at all dependent on the spiritual stature of the one gifted. Theirs is an objective ministry, whereas God's ultimate purpose in man is a subjective one, through the formation of the Spirit within him, and not merely by his temporary abode upon him. So gifts are called "spiritual," not because the recipient is spiritual but because they come from the Holy Spirit.

Why is it that so many who have been greatly used often seem later to be set aside? In reply to that question I would first of all ask: How do we know that God *wanted* always to use them in that kind of way? May he not have had other plans? For God signs no contracts! And after all, do we not ourselves often employ a servant for a few days on an urgent task, well aware that he is unproved or inexperienced, and with no guarantee of keeping him on for ever, untrained, in that particular service? We reserve the right to make changes. May it not be that God similarly uses men for a time, and then, in his wisdom, changes the nature of their employment?

God *lends* his strength, and it remains a divine loan, never to become our possession. Samson, for example, had the gift of strength. It seemed there was nothing he could not do. Yet in spiritual understanding or purity of life, he was of small account before God. Remaining foolish he yielded to compromise, and so compassed his own downfall. When we compare him with Samuel who followed him, we see that God could only use him to fulfill an immediate purpose; no more than that.

It is thus a mistake to measure spirituality merely by the presence of gifts. By themselves they are an inadequate basis for a man's lasting usefulness to God. They may be present and they may be valuable, but the Spirit's object is something far greater—to form Christ in us through the working of the Cross. His goal is to see Christ inwrought in believers. So it is not merely that a man does certain things or speaks certain words, but that he is a certain kind of man. He himself *is* what he preaches. Too many want to preach without being the thing themselves, but in the long run it is what we are, and not simply what we do or say, that matters to God; and the difference lies in the formation of Christ within.

GOD'S GIFT OF MEN

In 1 Corinthians 12 Paul defines three subjects with which he sets out to deal, namely, gifts and the Spirit (verse 4), ministrations and the Lord (verse 5), workings and God (verse 6). These three correspond, I think, in a general way to the subjects treated in the following sections of the chapter: gifts with verses 7-11, ministries with verses 12-27 (the passage we have already considered in some detail), and workings with verses 28 and 29, and it will be noted that in the third instance priority is given to the men concerned—apostles, prophets, teachers.

The Spirit gives gifts; God gives men. Here is a distinction that I think we do well to notice. It is of course the special emphasis of Ephesians 4 (see verses 11 and 12), but the whole tenor of Paul's writings, and not least here in 1 Corinthians, is upon the character of the men whom God can use.

If we are content to emphasize only gifts and the teaching of truth, and to stop short there, we can be sure of blessing and fruit—on that level. But is that enough? Do we want merely to be used? Samson was used. So were Balaam and Saul—for a time. But tell me, does what they represent satisfy us? Saul was but a temporary king; Balaam a temporary prophet. For it is not just a question of their words or acts, but of the men themselves. It is worth noting that when Jesus quoted the Old Testament he did not say "the prophecy of Isaiah" but "the prophet Isaiah." It is not "Ye have rejected the prophecies" but "Ye have rejected the prophets." The Lord lays great emphasis on the men. Not to receive the prophets or the apostles is not to receive the God who sent them.

This, I believe, should be the basis of our training. Some people have expressed surprise that young men and women desiring to serve the Lord come to us in Shanghai, when we offer no courses of lectures in Bible knowledge and homiletics, or similar subjects. But our hope is that those who come may become better men; not merely that they may learn more doctrine or acquire greater skill as preachers. The need is not for greater gifts, but for men whom God can use. Too often others are helped by our gifts, but hindered by what we are. The living water has had to content itself with unclean vessels. There is shame in that.

It is of course true that God does take up those who are not worthy and permit them to speak his words years before they fully understand their import, but he does not wish any of us to stop there. We may go on in that way for a while, but is it not true that, from the time when he begins in us his work of formation through discipline and chastening, it growingly dawns on us how little in fact we knew of the true meaning of what we had been saying? He intends that we should reach the place where we can speak, with or without manifest gifts, because we *are* the thing we say. For in Christian experience the spiritual things of God are less and less outward, that is, of gift, and more and more inward, of life. In the long run it is the depth and inwardness of a work that counts. As the Lord himself becomes more and more to us, other things—yes, and this must include even his gifts—matter less and less. Then, though we teach the same doctrine, speak the same words, the impact on others is very different, manifesting itself in an increasing depth of the Spirit's work within them also.

To his servants God gives the gift of prophecy; to the Church he gives prophets. And a prophet is one who has a history, one who has been dealt with by God, one who has experienced the formative work of the Spirit. We are sometimes asked by would-be preachers how many days should be spent in preparation of a sermon. The answer is: At least ten years, and probably nearer twenty! In this matter the proverb is true: "The old is better." For the preacher matters to God at least as much as the thing preached. God chooses as his prophets those in whom he has already worked what he intends to use as his message for today.

For to understand doctrine, and to know God, are two very different things. Spiritual things are never carried in the head. We lay weight upon good words, but God seeks good men. Some speak, and we are helped; others say the same words, and we are empty. The difference lies in the men themselves. We cannot deceive the Church with intellectual instead of spiritual values. The Church knows! Nothing can be a substitute for what a man is before God.

So the question is: Are we like the words we

say? "Lord, if I do not know thee, and the meaning of thy Cross, and the formative hand of thy Spirit upon me, save me from presumption in speaking, and begin in me today whatever work is needed to remedy the deficiency. Break, mold, test, try me, so that I may speak that which I know." This must be our cry; for to speak in his Name what we do not know will serve God, if at all, only a very little way.

GIFTS AND LIFE

"There are diversities of gifts, but the same Spirit. And there are diversities of ministrations, and the same Lord" (1 Cor. 12:4, 5). We have suggested already that the latter statement finds its parallel in the passage from verses 12 to 27 which deals with Christ and the mutual life of his Body. But in the two statements I think we can recognize another useful distinction, namely, that between gifts and life, between the means used for ministering and the thing ministered.

Gifts are the means received from the Holy Spirit by which I give of Christ to the Body; the ministry (or "ministration") is *what I give* of Christ to the Body. Each ministry contributes something more of Christ; and it is ministry rather than gifts that is compared here by Paul to the human body's functions of sight and hearing and movement. Thus, whereas different men may have the same gift, the same is not true of the different "ministries" of life suggested by the language of this passage. Each is peculiar—the unique life-contribution of each member to the whole. It is that which you or I have received specially from the Lord to share with his people, and it may even be something the Body has never before received. For the fulfilling of this ministry of "giving Christ," spiritual gifts are but the tools. I make use of them to give to the Body the Christ I know.

This is important, for it shows much so-called spiritual revival to have been on a wrong basis. Gifts are displayed, but without Christ, and that is like having many utensils but nothing to use them for. But it is worse, for without Christ, gifts are not only empty; they may also be deceptive. Some of them at least can be simulated in a way that a ministry of Christ can never be, whereas what matters to the Body is not our gifts, but the personal knowledge of Christ that we convey by them. In a hospital two nurses may use exactly similar spoons, but what they give in those spoons is the important thing; one may give costly and curative medicine, the other a mere palliative. It is *what* we minister that counts. The health and growth of the Body come from a ministry of Christ alone; they can never come merely from gifts as such. While gifts are needed (for "to each one is given the manifestation of the Spirit to profit withal") they are never a substitute for Christ. Our first duty is to ask ourselves "Have I anything to give?" and to learn by the Spirit how to give Christ to the Body.

How can I have a specific ministry? Not first by doctrine, but by life. Abraham learned faith in the place where only faith in God remained possible to him, not by being taught a doctrine. Abel learned in experience the value of forgiveness by blood. First come trouble, desperation, experience—*and life;* then afterwards doctrine. It is not in searching, studying, comparing, but at the place of desperation that God gives life. We should take every opportunity to study and learn, but therein we shall not find our ministry. Preachers are in special danger here, always looking for new light on the Scriptures, new themes for sermons. But the way to ministry does not lie there. Our special experience of Christ is what constitutes our ministry, and it is the trial of our faith that works in us experience.

At this point I would like to draw your attention to a significant change of emphasis that takes place in the writings of Paul himself, between his two letters to the Corinthians. 1 Corinthians, it seems, is occupied in the main with the ministry of gifts; 2 Corinthians with the ministry of life. In 1 Corinthians 12 and 14 many gifts are mentioned: wisdom, knowledge, healings, miracles, prophecy, discernment, tongues, interpretation and so on; and since these gifts are given for the good of the whole Church, the question mainly discussed there is: What is their special value? In 2 Corinthians 3 and 4 on the other hand, when Paul comes to speak of his own ministry, he does not emphasize gifts at all. He is clearly much more concerned about the formation of Christ within. Christ, the treasure in the vessel, is both the source and the theme of the ministry of the Church (2 Cor. 4:7). "Pressed, yet not straitened," "pursued, yet not forsaken," "smitten down, yet not destroyed," or as we might put it, "done for—and yet not done for!": it is the triumphant survival in Paul of *this treasure* that is the secret. The death of Christ working in him becomes the source of a life to be shared with the people of God.

We may paraphrase Paul's expression in verse 10, "the dying of Jesus" that I "bear about in the body," as: "the putting to death of Jesus that works death in me." This working of death is, as I have said elsewhere, something different from the once-for-all death of Romans 6, for it is a constant daily process in the child of God. And it leads first of all to life in me (verse 10). But—and here is our present point—it does not stop there, but goes on, praise God, to minister also *"life in you"* (verse 12).

Life, Paul tells us, is that with which he serves the Church, and in so saying he defines the thing upon which all true ministry in the Church is founded. Death, working in the servant of God, produces life; and because he has life, others too have life. The Church receives, because some are willing to bear the Cross. It is their reception of the death of Jesus that counts. This is Paul's new lesson for the Corinthians. By allowing God to work through their trials and testings, praising him and submitting to his will, his children make it possible for him to bring life to others. But only those who pay this price receive this costly ministry. For life is released through death, but only so. And whereas gifts by themselves are less costly, what gifts may enable us to do and say can never make good deficiencies in what we are as servants of God.

Thus we see two ministries by which the Body is built up—gifts and life; and we may ask ourselves: In which do we discern God's highest purpose? I reply: Not in gifts, but in the life from Christ which comes through death. Gifts are not to be dispensed with (1 Tim. 4:14; 2 Tim. 1:6; 1 Peter 4:10) but to set the greatest store by them is still to "think as a child" in spiritual things (1 Cor. 13:11). For it is in 2 Corinthians 3 and 4 that Paul points us forward to the thing most to be prized, and it is this, that out of our knowledge of Christ, acquired through the way he has led us, we minister to our brethren the life that the Spirit has formed in us.

Today, many minister by gifts; comparatively few by life. That may not be wrong where believers are young in the Lord, and where the measure of life through the working of the Cross in them is limited to the brief span of their spiritual history. Then, for the edification of young churches and the winning of souls, spiritual gifts may take on a special significance. But they are not in themselves a mark of maturity, and they are certainly never something of which to boast. Their display establishes faith, but with an increasing measure of spiritual life in the church, the need to depend upon them becomes less, and so does the danger of pride that accompanies them. Such progress does not mean that the things said or done are necessarily different, but that the meaning within God's servant grows. The words may not have altered, but they spring from a deeper inward consciousness. Not gifts, but the working of the Cross: this is the measure of a man's spiritual stature. Only the foolish are proud of the words God gives, for has he not shown that he will speak, if need be, through an ass!

In a sense, then, whether or not we use gifts is secondary. The important thing is that we minister life—the life we receive from the Lord. And whether or not God allows individuals to retain certain gifts, and to increase them, is his affair. But one thing is certain, that in the progress of *his Church*, God makes ever greater use of life and less of gifts. At least in their more conspicuous manifestations, gifts tend to diminish, life to increase. For effective ministry to the Church neither speech, eloquence, miracles nor tongues are of first importance. God uses men as his mouthpieces for a time, and then, as far as these things go, he may choose to set them aside. But the life of the Body goes on. To trust in gifts is therefore folly, unless they minister life from the Giver of life.

THE ATTACK ON THE CHURCH BY DEATH

While he was on earth Jesus was himself the vessel of divine life. When men touched him they touched God; when they saw him they saw God. All the fullness of the Godhead dwelt in him in bodily form (Col. 1:19; 2:9). Today that divine life is entrusted to the Church, his Body. She is the vessel of that life, destined to be filled unto all the fullness of God (Eph. 1:23; 3:19). All that is of Christ is intended to be seen in the Church. This is the purpose for which she has been left here by God. She is to contain and to display the life of his Son.

He is the Light, the Way, the Truth; he is the Son, the King, the "I AM." But what is his most distinctive role? In John 11:25 he tells us: "I am the resurrection and the life." Surely this is the feature most characteristic of him; and, as the opening chapters of the Book of Revelation show us, the Church is to know him thus, as the risen and living One, so that she too may bear this same character. Her task is to manifest the life and resurrection of Christ.

From Eden onwards, God's controversy with Satan has been on this issue of death and life. (See for example Gen. 3:3, 4; Rom. 5:12, 17, 21; 1 Cor. 15:22.) All of God is characterized by life, all of Satan by death. It is not only a question of holiness. There is much false holiness in the world, and we can readily be deceived by it, but life is one thing that cannot be simulated. Is there life in me? Do I touch life in another? These are the questions. For life is something deeper than thought, more real than feeling and doctrine. Where there is life there is God. The great difference between Christ and all others is that, whereas others are dead, he lives. Death could not touch him. And God who destroyed death through Christ, now uses the Church for the same purpose. Today she is God's vessel of life, called to reveal the risen life of his Son, and to bring men to the knowledge of that life.

But if this is the Church's work and ministry,

we can readily see what will be the nature of Satan's attack upon her. Death will be his weapon. Note the importance of this. If the attack came by way of sin, or the world, or by direct assault only, we should know how to guard against it. But even when the question of sin is settled, and even if the world has no attractions for us, yet Satan still has power. It is no use stopping one hole if the vessel has several others!

Sin is but the road; death is the goal. To deal with sin is still not to have touched death. If you have already arrived at a place, the destruction of the road thither does not get you away from that place. Satan's power lies not just in the love of the world, or sin, or in any kind of direct assault, whether on mind or body or anything else. We may overcome all these things and yet not be overcomers for he still has power through death.

Praise his Name, God has shown us right from the outset from what quarter the attack upon the Church will come. We are to expect it from "the gates of Hades"—that is, of death. This expression occurs only once in the New Testament, but there in Matthew 16:18 it is in its right place. Satan's greatest fear with regard to the Church is of her resistance, not to sinning, or to the love of the world, or to any of his direct attacks, but to his power of death.

For Satan's power was through death, and wherever he has dominion, it is death you touch. Neither demon-possession nor sin are his most characteristic works, but death. For this reason, the work of Christ could not stop short at redemption. The heart of his work was to bring to nought *through death* him who had the power of death (Heb. 2:14). This fact is a very great one. In the death of Jesus Christ, Satan's power of death met its match once for all. That death out-dies all other deaths. Death in Adam does not finish a man, but death in Christ does; it is a mighty death. In Christ all those who deserve to die have died, with the result that he who had the power of death no longer has dominion over them; they are dead. And ashes are something of which you can never make a fire. If a house is once burned to ashes there is no way of repeating the performance, for if the first fire has done its work, there is nothing for the next to do.

So the controversy between life and death that began in Eden ended in Gethsemane and at Calvary. There death was abolished, and life and immortality brought to light. Not only is Satan destroyed, but for us redeemed sinners, because we have already died a death in Christ, death too is gone, and we have become possessors of his incorruptible life.

Yet we should not regard the controversy as concluded even there. If "the gates of Hades" suggest a force, "shall not prevail" implies a continuing campaign. It is still in progress today. Satan's special object today is to spread death within the Church. In this little while, death is still his power. If he can bring death to the people of God now, he is satisfied; nor does he mind how much virtue there is so long as, with it, death is also present and active.

"The mind of the flesh is death; but the mind of the spirit is life and peace.... So then, brethren, we are debtors, not to the flesh, to live after the flesh: for if ye live after the flesh, ye must die; but if by the spirit ye mortify the deeds of the body, ye shall live" (Rom. 8:6 ff.). Words such as these, addresses as they are to believers, warn us to keep ourselves in life. But leaving aside sin, whose reward is death anyway, how many of us realize that to be merely passive in respect of life is to be a spreader of death? For in so doing we are giving room to the flesh.

Take a familiar example. There is no such spreader of death as scandal and criticism, *no matter how true to facts it be*. God wants us silent, but our tongue must work! He wants us quiet with him, but our legs keep going! To go when he wants us to stay, or to gossip when he wants us silent, these things spring from the lust of the flesh, just as truly as do its cruder manifestations. To bring the flesh—even "neutral" flesh—into God's work is to invite attack from the gates of Hades, and if we speak when God does not require it, be sure there is death in our words.

Life cannot be explained. When we touch it, we know it is life. But how? Not by thought or feeling or a "sixth sense." Those who know, know. Those who don't, don't. Those who know can never explain to those who don't—until they themselves know. Those who know life recognize it in others. Those who have death in themselves recognize neither life nor death. The natural man may discern between warmth and coldness, good doctrine and bad, but not between life and death. Many think that if nothing goes visibly wrong in the Church, then all is well. But to be thus unable to discern what is life and what is death is a fatal lack. We shall not know when we are being attacked. May God grant us this discernment!

Because it is the earthly expression of Christ and is so precious to him, the Church is the scene in which, if he could, Satan would stage a comeback, and for us to scatter death there is to be found cooperating with him. Alas, all that some of us do is just that! All our boasted "ability" in the work of God becomes a tool in his hands. Our natural genius and brilliance, unrestrained by the Cross, brings death to the Church. Even our sound doctrine, if seized upon by the natural mind—yes, and our spiritual "gift" too, if held and misused by the carnal man— spreads only death there. Remember Samson! Nothing that is not truly of God, the Fount of Life, can minister aught but death. In short, wherever men touch me rather than Christ in me, there they touch death and not life.

In this matter pretense is of no avail. The truth will out. For other things can be simulated, but life never. And as our spirit is, so is the impression we make. If death is there, death is what men meet; if life, then life.

This spreading of life or death is a present fact, in the home, the church, the prayer-gathering— everywhere. It is easier to preach when some are present, harder when others are there. Why? It has nothing to do with the persons. It all depends upon the pouring in or the draining away of life. Since the Body is the expression of Christ, only by ministering Christ can we contribute to the Body; and Christ is life. Those with life minister Christ in meetings. Others—even their "Amen" is dead! The spiritual power of the gatherings for Breaking of Bread and for prayer depends on whether those present are merely negative, or are bringing in life. For here in this age is still echoed the controversy fought out in Eden and at Calvary. Is resurrection life present? That is the question everywhere. Every member has a responsibility before God to bring into his house a ministry of the risen Christ.

MINISTERING LIFE TO THE BODY

The fact to which we find ourselves repeatedly brought back is that the Body of Christ is one. We cannot escape that fact, and Paul throws it once again into relief when he says: "And whether one member suffereth, all the members suffer with it; or one member is honored, all the members rejoice with it" (1 Cor. 12:26).

It is important to note carefully what is said here. If one member suffers, what we are told is not that all the members ought to suffer, but that they actually *do* suffer with it. Nor is it said that if one member is honored all the others ought to, but that they actually *do*, share the honor. If the oneness of the Body is not a fact, then these are no more than just beautiful sentiments. But because the oneness of the Body is a divine fact, it is also a fact that all the other members suffer with the suffering member. It is not just that they try to, or ought to, but that they actually do.

Verse 26 is to be read, not as guidance or exhortation to Christians how to act, but as a statement of what in fact takes place. Because the Body is eternally one, the whole suffers when the member suffers, and the whole is uplifted when the member is uplifted.

The children of God are sometimes made aware of this as a matter of experience. A dear friend of mine in South China told me of her sense of deep spiritual burden at the time of outbreak of the Boxer rising elsewhere in the country, the news of which had not yet filtered through to her district, and again of a sense of life and uplift of spirit during the Welsh revivals in Britain, of the occurrence of which she was otherwise quite uninformed. Another friend whom I visited in the West surprised me, when I spoke to him of a particularly severe time of testing in our work in China, by saying, "Of course we felt the reaction here some time before your letters reached us."

But whether we are informed of such things or not is not the point. The fact is that whenever there is a movement on the part of the Lord, there is a reaction on the part of the Body, and all the members are subject to that reaction. Our awareness of it depends not upon information but upon our knowledge of the Lord by the Spirit of life.

If a member of the Body commits some grievous sin, or is subject to some great suffering, the spiritual members will surely feel the pressure. Conversely, if a fresh influx of life comes to any member, other members who are vitally in the life of the Body will as surely know an uplift. At times you may go through great travail before you receive revelation from God; at other times light breaks in without your seeking it. In the first case, I suggest, you are breaking through to a fresh influx of life that is to be ministered to others; in the second you are reaping the benefit of the sufferings of others through which increase has come spontaneously to the Body as a whole.

But there is another side to this. If you are one who seeks increase for personal ends, you are cutting off the flow of life to yourself from the whole Body; and should you attain the increase you seek, not only will it not profit you, it will be actually detrimental both to yourself and to the rest of the Body besides. The counterpart in the physical body of such a condition is the disease we call cancer. Cancer results from the over-development of one cell. That one cell multiplies itself without restraint or control, and in doing so consumes all the nourishment that comes its way, instead of passing it on to the rest of the body. Functioning as a separate unit, it encroaches on the tissues around, imposing its own distorted character upon them. And whereas the spontaneous working of nature tends to correct other diseases, it is no correction for cancer, for the more life the body pours into the diseased area the more the cancer absorbs for its own advantage. Because the outflow is arrested, all inflow only increases the trouble. How true this is of spiritual things! In the normal course, a fresh influx of life coming to any

member of the Body instantly ministers increase
to the whole; but if one member becomes isolated through desire for personal gain, then the
more the member grows, the greater the menace
to the whole Church of Christ.

How precious therefore is the Cross of Christ!
It lies within the scope of every single member to
raise the tide of life in the whole Body, provided
he will let the Cross deal drastically with the life
of nature in him. For the Body's sake let us pray:
"Lord, shatter in me all that is selfishly individual and that will weaken thy Body, and for
the sake of thine own increase, cause me to touch
realms of life never touched before!"

We have seen already how, in 2 Corinthians 4,
the death of Christ operating in one place ("in
the body," verse 10; "in us," verse 12) allows
him to manifest his resurrection in two places
("in our body," verse 10; and "in you," verse 12).
Here we have fruitfulness of life and fruitfulness
of ministry, and of course they are ultimately
one, the only difference being in the place of
manifestation. In the first instance, the life is
manifested in the place where death operates; in
the second, somewhere else. When the manifestation is in me I call it life, when in others I call it
ministry.

Where there is no Cross there is no life, and no
ministry of life. The object of suffering is that
there may be a full and abundant ministry.
Theory is no substitute for this. Poverty of ministry results from the choice of an easy road. Those
who have an easy time all too often have little to
give. They do not understand men's needs. Of

course I don't mean we are to invite trouble, or by austerity to ill-treat our bodies. The Spirit himself takes responsibility for our experience, leading us in paths where we encounter, in body, heart, or spirit, that measure of "the dying of Jesus" that will mean enrichment to our ministry. It is our part only to follow.

You ask me how you can be used to minister life to the Body. Not by setting out deliberately to do a lot, nor indeed by running away into retirement and doing nothing, but simply by letting the Cross operate in the normal course of your walk with the Lord. Those who only serve by words and works find they have no ministry if at any time they are reduced to inactivity or silence. But the measure of your ministry is not determined by the measure of your activity. Only let "the slaying of Jesus" work in you, and life *must* manifest itself in others. It cannot be otherwise, for it is an abiding principle of the Body that "death worketh in us, but life in you." So you need make no special effort to bring increase to the Body in this way, or anything God takes you through by way of the Cross will spontaneously bring increase there.

Nor need you talk a lot, for it is not necessary to testify to your death experience in order for it to become vital to others. Provided you are willing for death, others *will* know life. Reality communicates itself; it is not dependent upon human communications. We "despise not prophesyings," but we affirm nevertheless that ministry in the Body is not only a question of preaching or testifying. What we go through in secret with the Lord is quite sufficient to minister life to his members. If we suffer for the Lord's sake, that suffering will bring increase to others, without our making known the story of our suffering. Talking about it is not only superfluous; in some circumstances it is an abomination.

If you forgive a brother, the reality of your forgiveness will minister life to the Body quite apart from my expression of it (though in this case the Lord may of course require of you that it be expressed). If you truly love a brother, that love will build up the Body though you may never tell that brother how you love him. I found myself once, at short notice, taking part on the platform in a large convention meeting in England where, unknown to me, a Japanese brother was to be one of the speakers. We had not met before—and our two countries were at war. I do not know what that brother felt, and we had opportunity for only a brief conversation. I only know that while he spoke I was aware of the love and fellowship of a brother in the Lord, a love that leaped over national barriers and that did not demand words for its expression.

The Body of Christ is ministered to, not first of all by preaching and working, but by inward reality. The Holy Spirit is concerned with what is real and true, and will never witness to what is not real. What you communicate by words is what you are already bringing of Christ to the Church, for as we have said, the Body is ministered to by a communication of life. And life is communicated to others, quite simply and spontaneously, as death operates in us. So the question is not, How much are you doing or saying? but, How much are you going through under the hand of God?

Ministry on any basis other than the oneness of the Body is unreal. Until you have seen that fact, you constantly wonder how you can function; but when you see it, you know that as soon as you yourself have received something, the Body *has* received it. What is yours *is* the Body's, and there is no need to struggle to pass it on. Do you want to build up the church? Then let it be built up in you. What you receive from the Head, the Church, his Body, spontaneously receives; and what you have not received, it can never receive through you. The question of ministry is settled when the question of receiving is settled; and the question of receiving is settled by "the dying of Jesus."

WORDS THAT ARE SPIRIT AND LIFE

Of course there is a place—and a great need— for the ministry of the Word. We can, if we like, classify spiritual gifts into gifts of *work* or action (such as healings, miracles) and of *word* (such as prophecy, teaching, tongues, and so forth), and if we do so I think we shall discover that Paul tends to lay his main stress on the latter. Whatever they may possess of other gifts, all the three classes of men—apostles, prophets, teachers— that head his list in 1 Corinthians 12:28 are surely, first of all, ministers of the Word of God. We are told for example that this, together with prayer, was the main concern of the Twelve when they sought release from the administrative tasks to "continue ... in the ministry of the word" (Acts 6:4). So Paul concludes his comments on this list with the exhortation to "desire earnestly the greater gifts," and then, returning to the subject after his intervening discourse on love, adds: "but rather that ye may prophesy" (12:31; 14:1). Indeed Chapter 14 that follows is quite taken up with gifts of speech, and passes over miracles or gifts of action altogether.

So for the building up of his Church, God emphasizes the ministry of the Word above the ministry of works. The Church is not to trust in miracles, for they may only lead to outward things. Israel in the wilderness continually touched God's works, but missed his life. So did the multitudes in the Gospels, who witnessed the Lord's gracious acts but knew nothing of the life he came to give. Even the disciples fell short here, for having performed miracles themselves, they fell at last to arguing who of them should be the greatest. Here was no building in love!

But "the seed is the word." Apart from God's Word of life, nothing counts for much. Miraculous works may support the Word; they cannot by themselves minister life. It is by the eternal Word of the Lord that the Church must grow.

Many ills of the Church today spring from the fact that Christians are content with a merely objective acceptance of doctrine. They seek an outward, mental light on the Scriptures, but stop short of a subjective application of the Word of God to experience. They find many mental difficulties in the Bible, and light, to them, is the solving of these. For many, general truth has taken the place of specific truth. They feel that all is well if they are "conservative" or "orthodox" in their doctrine, and give mental assent to this and mental dissent from that. By this reasoning, fundamentalists consider themselves on a far higher plane than modernists; yet they measure up spiritually in God's eyes only in so far as they possess a true inward revelation of Christ, and no further. They may be perfectly *right*, but unless they possess life, they lack the one supreme essential.

Today the Church has the letter of the Word, and we praise God that she does! We have our Bibles and our translations, and we thank him for them all. But the letter—even the fundamental letter—kills; it is only the Spirit that gives life (2 Cor. 3:6). If we are to bring life to others, we must not only preach the Word according to God's thought of centuries ago; we must know also how the Spirit applies that Word to men today.

For a "prophet" in the New Testament is one who, like Elijah or John the Baptist, proclaims God's present purpose for his people. His preaching is of the utmost importance, because it brings to light through the Word the mind of God for his own day. Three things characterize a prophet: a history before God, an inward burden, and divinely-given words that express and interpret that burden, so that having ministered the Word he returns home with his burden gone.

For such a ministry today the study of the Scriptures is essential. Of course, any reasonably intelligent person can learn a lot of the Bible in a year, but if we are serious with him, God will not let that pass without taking steps to ensure that what we are tallies with what we say. For understanding of the Scriptures comes in two ways, one merely from study, the other from knowing and following the Lord himself, and there is a vast difference between the two. On the mere level of the understanding of doctrine, a graduate in theology may be able to systematize perfectly for you all that the Scriptures contain. Yet he will not be proclaiming the Word until that Word has come to him directly from God, and he has responded. Another man, with no knowledge of theology as a science, may yet minister out of a deep knowledge of God, because God speaks to him through the Word, and because whenever God does so, he unquestioningly obeys.

When a brother stands up and speaks, you know at once whether he stresses doctrine or life. If it is the former, he never runs risks. He keeps carefully within the limits of his doctrinal system, in order to be absolutely safe and to avoid all possible chance of misunderstanding. He presents his many reasons in logical order, and at length, by a process of induction, arrives at his incontrovertible conclusion. But one who stresses life will be far less concerned with technical correctness, or with the exhaustive treatment of his subject. His approach will be a quite different one, for he has himself known conditions through which doctrine alone could never carry him. If only, therefore, he can fulfill his one object, which is to present Christ to his hearers, he will not feel the absolute need to produce for this purpose a fully logical and fool-proof case.

For the Bible itself is not like that. In his Word God has never given us a completely systematic setting forth of any doctrine—never, that is, as we understand system. The Bible does not reach its conclusions by induction, and there are in it many passages capable of being misunderstood. Sometimes, I am afraid, we may almost dare to feel that, had we been writing it, we would have put things far more plainly! The great spiritual facts, the mighty eternal truths of God, seem often half obscured in his Word, so that the natural man cannot easily discover them. Nevertheless, through the Spirit, things hidden from the wise and prudent have been revealed to babes. Blessed be God, that has been his way! Salvation, righteousness by faith, sanctification, life—do we know these things merely as doctrinal themes, or as actualities? God's thought is not that we should only grasp them with our minds, but that we should experience them in life.

A vast knowledge of the Bible will not make up for a little knowledge of the Lord. We must know *him*, and the Bible as *his* Word, the expression of his present mind in regard to his people. You ask, *Can* we know the mind of God? Yes indeed, for God has not withdrawn himself. He still speaks through the Scriptures as he always did, even today when the Church is so sadly defeated. He still chooses those with a history before him, to be his spokesman in their generation. In an hour when men are so largely unconcerned about divine things, the Church's desperate need is of men with such knowledge.

God seeks true ministry in his saints. That is why we have such bad times! We must not question it if he leads us into the unexpected, for when he does so, we can be sure it is with some definite goal in view. For the ministry to the Body of a personal knowledge of Christ can lift every member onto a new spiritual plane. Perhaps our greatest service to the Lord would be to make way for him to do the unprecedented with us, and so make possible a new enrichment of life for the entire Body of Christ.

Should we not, therefore, gladly place ourselves in his hands, that we may be found with some definite discovery of Christ to contribute? "Lord, may I receive from thee some measure of life that the Body has never before received, that thy people may be enriched and thy heart satisfied!"

9
Gathered in the Name

In earlier chapters we have placed strong emphasis upon the unity of the Church. Always and only have we seen her as one and undivided. Now we have to ask ourselves a question: Is there any point at which this view of her has to be qualified? For does not Scripture speak not alone of "the Church" but also of "the churches"? Where and at what point does the Church of God become the churches of God?

If we look carefully into this, we shall discover that the basis of division (if we can use that word at all) is a single one—that of locality alone. If the New Testament is to be our guide, the *only* ground of division contemplated is geographical. There is in the Word of God no room for the grouping of Christians together into things called "churches" on such grounds, for example, as history or doctrine, mission-connection or personal allegiance, or even a special message or ministry. The names given to churches in Scripture are invariably those of cities, that is, of local centers of community life. We read of "the church of God which is in Corinth," "the church of the Thessalonians," "the seven churches that are in Asia" (each, of course, named after a single city), and so forth. It is such expressions alone that designate the Church of God distributed on earth, and Scripture knows no exceptions.

But this brings us to another thing, and it is this, that the very same word "church" is used locally as is used universally (for of course in Greek there is no distinction by capitals and lower case). We read of "the Church which is his Body" but we read also "the church of God which is at Corinth" and "the church in thy house" (Eph. 1:23; 1 Cor. 1:2; Philemon 2). Surely this means that the church in a locality *is* the Church which is his Body (with all the profound wealth of meaning that goes into that term) finding her local expression in that place at that time.

But if this last statement is true, it places an altogether new emphasis upon one thing of which we may till now have missed the significance, namely, the importance to God of the present local expression of the Body comprising all the members of Christ in any one place. In Corinth or Laodicea, Rome or Lystra, all the members of Christ by new birth were called upon to function against the secular background as an expression of the one Body. Every dividing of them up on other principles would only touch their life and testimony adversely.

Leaving aside, of course, the more limited grouping together of brothers and sisters for special tasks in the work of the Lord, I affirm again that the Church embraces all the believers; it has no room for sectarian alliances. It was one of the reproaches held against the church in Corinth that parties had begun to appear there claiming personal allegiances. Today that kind of thing has become perpetuated in various ways, but to this Paul's challenge is as strong and clear now as it was then: "Is Christ divided? Was Paul crucified for you? or were ye baptized in the name of Paul?"

In a passage at the end of Romans touching on the subject of church life, the apostle begins his discussion with the words "God hath received him," and ends it with "Christ also received us" (14:3; 15:7). Here is the simple basis of all our life and fellowship with others. It is that they belong to the Lord, and so do we. That is sufficient. We do not join with them because they and we belong to the same denomination or owe our Christianity to the same mission, nor because both share a liking for a certain preacher or his message, nor yet because they hold particular doctrinal views and we hold the same views, nor even because they have had a certain Christian experience and we have had a like experience. No, we join with them solely and sufficiently because they belong to the Lord and we too belong to the same Lord. It is in him that we are one.

It is not my desire here to attack denominational Christianity as wrong. I only say again that, for the Body of Christ to find effective local expression, the basis of fellowship must be a true one. And that basis is the life-relation of the members to their Lord and their willing submission to him as Head. Nor am I pleading for those who will make a fresh sect of something called "localism"—that is, the strict demarcation of churches by localities. For such a thing could easily happen. If what we are doing today in life becomes tomorrow a mere method, so that by its very character some of his own are excluded from it, may God have mercy upon us and break it up! For all those in whom the Lord, the Spirit, has liberty are ours and we are theirs. No, I am pleading only for those who will see the heavenly Man, and who in their life and fellowship will follow after that! Christ is the Head of the Body—not of other "bodies" or units of religion. Involvement in the spiritual Body of Christ is what secures the committal of the Head to us, his members—that, and that alone.

"CONCLUDING THAT GOD HAD CALLED US"

We must now consider this matter of divine committal to the Church along three lines—

those of guidance, discipline, and prayer. God has made a threefold provision for our guidance in the Christian pathway: we have the Holy Spirit, we have the Word of God, and we have the Body of Christ. The Word of God shows me the will of God for me; the Holy Spirit reveals the will of God in me; the Body, by putting that will into the larger perspective of the divine purpose, shows me how it is to affect my relationships as a member. (This will, no doubt, recall what we said earlier about the twofold will of God, "A and B.") Unhappily, because of our reaction against the tyranny of Rome which has made so much of the political world-Church, we are inclined to discard altogether the third of these divine gifts. But every error arises out of a distortion of truth. The truth here is that the Body *is* one, and that fellowship in the Body remains an essential factor in my spiritual illumination. I must know the mind of God, not only by the Word of God to me, nor yet alone by the Spirit of God in me, but together with both of these, by taking also my place among God's people in his house.

We would all agree that there is such a thing as individual prayer and there is also such a thing as Church prayer. But equally there is such a thing as light given to the individual and there is also such a thing as light given to the Church. Is it not true that, without the nature of our problem being known to anyone, we often receive light in a church meeting that we cannot discover at home with the Word? Why is this? Surely because the Church is the House of God, the place of manifestation of divine light. Outside we may have the light of nature, but in the sanctuary there is no light, natural or artificial, save the Shekinah of God himself.

This principle of fellowship in guidance was one of the foundations of Paul's life and ministry. We see it in Acts 13, where, as with several others he is found waiting on the Lord, the Holy Spirit says to them "Separate me Barnabas and Saul for the work whereunto I have called them." We said earlier that the anointing of the Spirit is given for the personal guidance of every individual believer, and in keeping with this, we know that on at least two occasions Saul had earlier received a personal call of God to go to the Gentiles (Acts 26:16-18; 22:21). But now the time and way of that leading forth is revealed to several together. Luke says, "they sent them away," but he also describes them as "sent forth by the Holy Ghost" (13:3, 4). Here we have the Church and the Spirit acting in conjunction, the initiative of the one Spirit being expressed in the one Body.

Again, at the end of chapter 15 we find Paul and Silas being "commended by the brethren to the grace of the Lord" as they set out for Syria and Cilicia. Though it is never safe to argue from silence, it may be significant that the going forth of Barnabas to Cyprus, which is not covered by a similar statement of commissioning by the Church but seems to have been a more personal move, takes him also at that point out of the Scripture record (verses 36-41).

A little later, in Troas, a vision appeared to

Paul: "Come over into Macedonia and help us," and after describing it Luke goes on: "We sought to go forth ... concluding that God had called us to preach the gospel unto them" (16:9, 10). The Lord often gives a vision to an individual, but the movement is not based on that individual alone. It is based on a corporate seeking of God. And in this passage too it is the Holy Spirit who takes the initiative (verses 6, 7). It is because we move with the Holy Spirit that we are found moving with the Body. The real test of the vision will always be that the Spirit of truth witnesses to it.

"RESTORE SUCH A ONE"

In Matthew chapter 18 the Lord tells me how I may need to be rebuked by a brother, and how when he comes, if I decline to heed what he says, the point may be reached where the witness of the church as a whole needs to be called in to bring me to see my error. (Or of course the situation may be reversed, and my brother be the offender.) The thought immediately presents itself: How totally out of place it is for one sinner to discipline another! If we are to have any part or lot in such a ministry of correction, it can never be on the ground of our superiority to those with whom we seek to deal. They and we have alike sinned, and our hope in dealing with them is that there may be shown to them by God the same grace that has been shown to us.

Now suppose, in the example given, you are the offended party, then you are also the one appointed to deal with the offender. How are you going to do it? To flare up and vent your wrath on him will be to treat him as an enemy, remote from you. But just to forgive him and ignore the whole affair will be no better. You are treating him instead as a stranger and an inferior, for thereafter, whenever he sees you he remembers that he has wronged you, and whenever you see him you remember that you have behaved magnanimously in forgiving him.

No, he is your brother, and your attitude towards him is to be that of a brother dealing with a brother. You should treat the matter exactly as you would had the offense been committed against someone else and not against yourself. Deal with the case as if you were a third party (like the brother who may be called in later to help you if the need arises). And the Lord states very clearly what is to be your object in doing so. It is not the winning of your case, but to be told, "Thou hast gained thy brother."

We are to take this clause, surely, as covering the whole incident. That is to say, if your brother does not respond, and you are compelled to take two or three others with you as witnesses and seek him out again, your attitude is to be no different. It is still one, not of bringing a charge, but of seeking to win a brother. And in the extreme case where the whole church has to be called in, there is even then to be no change of purpose. The goal of the discipline remains that brother's restoration. Even one in spiritual advance of another dare not take a "better-than-thou" position, standing as one on a superior level to correct an inferior.

"Ye which are spiritual," says Paul, "restore such a one in a spirit of meekness; looking to thyself, lest thou also be tempted" (Gal. 6:1).

This brings us a step further, for our passage in Matthew 18 proceeds with these significant words about the authority of the members together: "What things soever ye shall bind on earth shall be bound in heaven: and what things soever ye shall loose on earth shall be loosed in heaven" (verses 15-18). What is this? It is not the tyranny of the church's overseers, nor is it the verdict of the majority over the minority. It is the church arising to purge the church.

The discipline of a member should never be a mere matter of business; rather should it be one of heart concern for the whole church. It is an abominable thing to see the disciplining of any child of God carried through in a trifling manner, as though it were a light thing; but it is no less abominable to see it carried through as a serious matter, if the seriousness is only that of a law-court. No discipline should be without grief and tears on the part of those who exercise it, nor can it ever be if they have recognized what the Church is. Paul wrote: "There is fornication *among you*." He did not, in the first place, locate that sin in any individual believer; he located it in the church. And he wrote: "Ye are puffed up, and did not rather mourn" (1 Cor. 5:1, 2). The sin was the sin of the whole Body, and the shame and the sorrow should not be just of one member but of the whole.

In Church discipline we need to see the oneness of the Body of Christ, but we need also to see not just the fact but also the potentiality of sin. I must first locate *in myself* the sin that is manifest in my brother, and not till I have judged it in myself dare I judge it in him. By the grace of God I may not have committed the same act, but I have within me the sin that provoked that act.

Discipline is always a remedial measure, and has as its object the recovery of the sinning brother. Even in the most extreme case the end in view is "that the spirit may be saved in the day of the Lord Jesus" (1 Cor. 5:3-5). Where God's children are concerned, there is mercy in all his judgment; and when we judge any of his children on his behalf, whether we do so as the whole church or as individual members, we should be full of mercy. Even though our outward act may have to be one of discipline, our inner attitude should be one of love.

After his resurrection, our Lord said to his disciples, "Receive ye the Holy Spirit," and added immediately, "Whose soever sins ye forgive, they are forgiven unto them; whose soever sins ye retain, they are retained" (John 20:22, 23). Rome appropriated this falsely, and reacting against Rome, we repudiate it. But in doing so how much have we Protestants lost! And how much is God losing! For what belongs to the Church of God cannot be lightly thrown away. Though "the church" be but a handful of simple village believers gathering in a home, if they see themselves in Christ as an expression of his Body, and if, confessing before him their weakness, they claim his wisdom and power, the Lord stands by that. "For where two or three are gathered together in my name, *there am I.*"

THE LIMITATIONS OF GOD

We have seen guidance and discipline in the Church; we will turn now to the Church's prayer. As we have said, fundamentally there are two kinds of prayer. The first is individual and devotional. We find it repeatedly alluded to in John's Gospel in such promises as the following: "Whatsoever ye shall ask in my name, that will I do, that the Father may be glorified in the Son" (14:13; compare verse 14 and chapters 15:7; 16: 23, 24). There are no conditions here. It is a promise for every individual member of Christ, and it makes prayer a very great thing. If, in the light of such statements, God does not hear and answer our individual prayers, we may feel there is surely something wrong with them.

But the second kind of prayer both includes the first and goes beyond it. It is that described in our passage in Matthew 18: "Again I say unto you, that if two of you shall agree on earth as touching anything that they shall ask, it shall be done for them of my Father which is in heaven" (verse 19). This is the Church's task, her God-given ministry of prayer. For the promise here is conditional; there must be at least two, and they in agreement.

And why is their prayer answered? The next verse explains: "For where two or three are gathered together in my name, there am I in the midst of them." They "are gathered" (passive voice); they do not just meet. We see the differ-

ence, for to be gathered is not merely to go of
ourselves; it is to be moved by the Spirit, as they
were moved who gathered at Hebron to make
David king. And they come, not on their own
affairs, but having a single common concern for
his. It is this that unites them "into" his Name.
And when this is so, then "I am in the midst,"
leading, revealing, enlightening. And, praise
God, that is not a promise, it is a statement of
fact! We *know* when he is present, and that presence explains why two on earth have such
power.

God waits for the prayers of his children to
bring in his Kingdom. For if this age is important, the age that follows is infinitely more so.
All the privileges and power we enjoy now are
only a foretaste of the powers of the age to come.
The fullness of God that is hidden now will be
manifest then. In the light of this, we see the
importance of what we call "The Lord's Prayer."
For thousands of years God commanded his
people to pray, but through the centuries he gave
them no instruction as to what they should pray
about, apart from this one prayer.

"Thy kingdom come!" We are to pray for this.
If his Kingdom would come of itself, we should
not have been given that command. But God's
people are to pray, for his work is always done in
response to his people's cry. The Lord's prayer is
not just a model prayer for me; it is a revelation
of God's heart. "True prayer begins at the heart
of God, is made known to the hearts of men, is
prayed back to God again, and God answers."
That is more than a definition; it is, I believe, the

principle of God's working in the universe.

"Thy will be done!" Yes, but where? "On earth," for this is the only place where today God's will is not done. Then how can God's Kingdom be brought in down here? By the created will, in union with the Uncreated Will, seeking the displacement of the rebellious will of the devil. For prayer is always three-sided. It involves someone prayed to, someone prayed for, and someone prayed against; and on earth there is someone to pray against—a will that is opposed to God's. Against that rebellious will, God will not act alone. He awaits our prayers.

There are many passages in the Gospels which affirm that God has subjected himself to limitations. We find Jesus prevented from entering a Galilean city, or refused passage through a Samaritan village, or again, powerless to do any mighty work in Nazareth (Mark 1:45; Luke 9:53; Mark 6:5). "How am I straitened!" he could cry; "How often would I have gathered thy children ... and ye would not." "Ye will not come to me, that ye may have life." (Luke 12:50; Matt. 23:37; John 5:40.) So the grain of wheat has no other course than to "fall into the earth and die"; and still today the word of God must be sown "among thorns" (John 12:24; Matt. 13:22). The same thing continues on into the later New Testament history, as well as being found, of course, everywhere in the Old. The water of divine deliverance depends upon the provision of human ditches. The oil of the Spirit flows until "there is not a vessel more." "Behold, the Lord's hand is not shortened, that it cannot save; neither his ear

heavy, that it cannot hear: but your iniquities ..."
(2 Kings 3:16, 18; 4:6; Isaiah 59:1, 2).

How did it come about that Omnipotence became limitable by man? And will it continue
throughout eternity? For surely, God is El Shaddai, "God Almighty"; eternity past and eternity
to come hold nothing able to limit him, nothing
to arrest or hinder or delay.

But God has a will. He seeks communion with
a people who will share his life and manifest his
Son. To that end he created heaven and earth—
and man; and then the trouble started. For, in
keeping with his purpose, God had created man
a being with free will, and he has determined not
to accomplish that purpose without the free
cooperation of man's will. This is a solemn principle; none more so. It means that, whereas in
the eternities God was absolute, here in time he
has chosen, instead of compelling his creatures,
to limit his own omnipotence to their free
choice. Man has been given power to make way
for, or to obstruct, the power of God.

To such limitation God was prepared to subject himself, knowing the triumph of divine love
that would as a result be manifest in the future of
eternity. He works towards that goal. His glory is
that, in the ages to come, man's free will will be
one with the will of God. The omnipotence then
will be morally greater even than in eternity
past, because there will be a *possible* limitation.
Man will still be *able* to disobey, but he will
never choose to do so. The separate, created will
of man will be wholly set for God, and that is
glory.

We know the risk God was willing to run in order to gain this end, and that when man's first choice led him in a wrong direction, the Father sent the beloved Son to redeem the loss. Here was One whose will was absolutely identified with God's, and, praise God! through his death and resurrection and by the power of the Spirit, a Body was formed whose members will be no less committed to that Uncreated Will. In them the divine limitations will be for ever done away. The Church is to secure for God the release of his power into the world, by bringing it to bear on evil situations in the realm of the spirit, for their overthrow. The Church is—I speak reverently— to restore to God his own omnipotence.

Prayer is the present exercising of my will in God's favor; declaring that his will shall be done. For this is true prayer, that what God makes known, we express. Man wills something that God has already willed, and gives it utterance. We do not ask ourselves, "Is my prayer *according to* God's will?" but "*Is* it God's will?" The will of God is the starting-point; we voice it; God does it. And if we do not voice it, it will not be done. Our prayers thus lay the track down which God's power can come. Like some mighty locomotive, his power is irresistible, but it cannot reach us without rails. When men cease to pray, God ceases to work, for without their prayer he will do nothing. It is they who direct heaven's power to the place of need.

Read again Matthew 18:18-20 and see the tremendous range of the Church's responsibility in prayer. The measure of the Church is the measure of God in the earth today. As once he was revealed through Jesus himself in Jerusalem and Galilee, so now he is revealed through his Church wherever it is found worldwide. He cannot go beyond the extent of the Church, for the Church alone represents the coming race. She stands for God on the earth, and what she looses and binds, heaven looses and binds. On earth today God's power is as great as her prayers; no greater. All that he does in relation to his eternal purpose, he does through her, and where she falls behind in her work, to that extent he is limited.

The Church cannot increase God's power, but she can limit it. She cannot make him do what he does not will to do, but she can hinder that which he does will. There are many things that he would bind and loose in heaven—things which hinder to be bound, things of spiritual value to be loosed—but movement on earth must precede movement in heaven, and God always waits for his Church to move.

"What things soever": these are precious words. Here heaven is measured by earth, for there is always more power in heaven than the measure of our asking; there is always more to be loosed or bound in heaven than we ask down here. Why do we want deliverance from sin? Why do we cry to God for enduement? To pray, "Thy will be done in me" is a good beginning, but we must go on to "Thy will be done on earth." The children of God today are taken up with far too small things, whereas their prayer is intended for the release of heaven's mighty acts.

Prayer for myself or my own immediate concerns must lead on to prayer for the Kingdom. Here is the answer to the question: What is the ministry of the Church? She is to be heaven's outlet, the channel of release for heaven's power, the medium of accomplishment of God's purpose. Many things have accumulated in heaven because God has not yet found his outlet on earth; the Church has not yet prayed.

How is God to get this? How is he going to have his Church on his side? Only by every one of us remembering, in the solemn conditions of today, that this ministry of being God's outlet is our greatest possible work. God shows what he wants, we stand and ask, and God acts from heaven: this is true prayer, and this is what we must see fully expressed in our prayer meetings. If the Church here in Shanghai, not to speak of other places, does not know this ministry of prayer, may God forgive us! Without it, all else is empty; God has no vessel here. "Not every one that saith unto me, Lord, Lord, shall enter into the kingdom of heaven; but he that doeth the will of my Father which is in heaven" (Matt. 7:21). With the Kingdom in view, all we have and all we are must be set for the will of God. God needs this. He must have a few throughout the nations who hold on in prayer, and who, by driving a wedge into the power of the enemy, bring in the next age. That is overcoming. Whether the members may be many or few, may God maintain our strength to work for him in deep, strong, prevailing prayer.

SPOILING THE STRONG MAN'S GOODS

"And ye shall chase your enemies, and they shall fall before you by the sword. And five of you shall chase an hundred, and an hundred of you shall chase ten thousand: and your enemies shall fall before you" (Lev. 26:7, 8). This was the promise of God to Israel as a people; but in the event, the reckoning seems to have been even more astounding, for one is said to have chased a thousand, and two to have put ten thousand to flight (Deut. 32:30). Here surely is a picture of prayer, individual or corporate, alone or with two together. For where two agree on earth, heaven binds ten thousand foes. How often have the people of God, in an hour of crisis, taken these words of Jesus at their face value and proved them! So on the night when Peter lay in prison, the church throughout Jerusalem got to its knees and prayed earnestly, and all Herod's authority was as nothing before the response of heaven to that prayer. Another Kingdom had invaded his territory, and even the great prison door yielded and gave way of itself.

Another Kingdom had invaded his territory. To elaborate this statement, let me take an illustration from modern history. As most Westerners are aware, a century ago the great foreign powers trading with China used their force of arms to impose on the Chinese people a principle against which they have ever since harbored a deep resentment. I refer to what is usually termed "extraterritoriality." By this principle, areas of Chinese territory were ceded to the foreign powers, and the citizens of those powers were made immune from legal action by the Chinese authorities for any personal infringement of the laws of China. They could be tried only by a consul or other public functionary of their own country, and according to that country's foreign laws. It was a highhanded way of doing business, and today all recognize the imposition as having been unjust. Yet perhaps, without fear of misunderstanding, we may use it to illustrate something quite different and in no sense unjust, namely, the present invasion of this earth by heaven's gracious rule.

How does this illustration apply to us? It does so in two ways. First as to ourselves, God has "made us to be a kingdom" (Rev. 1:5, 6). As far as this world is concerned, we are citizens of a "foreign" power. Delivered from the kingdom of darkness we are no longer subject to the prince of this world, under whose sway it lies. Instead we own allegiance to another King and are subject to another law. As to our persons, we have "extraterritorial rights."

But second, as to this world itself, here too we have claims to make. For over it man was created to have dominion, and what he lost, the Son of man has recovered. Today, spiritual world rulers have usurped that dominion, and the Church's vocation is to reclaim it from them. Though he is its "prince," Satan is in fact a usurper—an illegal squatter on God's inheritance.

Suppose a man somehow gets into your house and occupies it without your authority. What do you do? You go to the magistrate, and, appealing

to the law of the land, you get a verdict against
him. You return armed with a court order, and
you turn him out. He may be fortunate not to go
out in chains! But the situation in this world is
no different. God's "statute book" has already
ruled against this world's illegal occupant. He is
to go! What matters it that in Satan's eyes the law
of the Kingdom of heaven is a "foreign" law?
Calvary has established the superiority of that
Kingdom. At the Cross, Christ overthrew Satan's
whole legal standing. Now it is the Church's task
to see that other law is put into effect. Crying to
God like the widow in the parable, "Avenge me
of my adversary!" she is to obtain the order for
his eviction, and throw him out. God waits for
that cry. In a given situation, and at his word, we
are to put down our foot on a piece of spiritual
territory occupied by evil powers, and to lay
claim to it for God.

What kind of men are needed for this task? I
say again: just simple believers, it may be only
two or three together, but with the Lord in the
midst. For we do not ourselves have to bind the
strong man—that is already done—but only to
remind him that he has no real escape from his
bonds! Let me illustrate by telling you a story.

In a certain city in China there were two sisters. They were unlearned, and, humanly speaking, not "bright," but they had known the Lord
for some while. One day they were confronted
with a woman possessed with a demon, violent
and dangerous, and in great distress. Having
sought the Lord together, they approached her,
and in the Name of Jesus commanded the demon

to go out. To their dismay, nothing happened, and their inclination was to go away and seek the help and advice of someone more experienced. But as they hesitated and lifted their hearts to the Lord, asking him what they should do, a sudden thought came to them. Going back and again addressing the evil spirit, they preached to it Jesus. At once, through the woman but in its own peculiar voice, the spirit replied, "Oh, yes, I know Jesus! I have worshiped him all my life!" And with that the possessed woman arose, and crossing the room pointed them to an idol shrine in the courtyard.

Then they understood! The demon was, as we say, "trying it on" with them. Now they knew what to do. Beginning again from the beginning: "Do you remember two thousand years ago," they said, "Jesus of Nazareth cast out many of your fellow demons, until at length they all turned on him and slew him? Nevertheless he rose again, stripping off principalities and powers, and is now exalted far above all rule and authority. And there was a proclamation made: In that Name every knee in heaven and on earth and under the earth shall bow! Do you remember? Now, in *that* Name we command you to go!" And the demon obeyed.

When I asked them afterwards from where they got this light, they could not explain. They could only say that the Lord himself had come to their aid and exposed the subtlety of the enemy. But this incident surely disposes of our question: What sort of people are needed for this task? The answer is that no sort of people can stand up to

Satan. Demons only recognize Christ. "If I by the Spirit of God cast out devils, then is the kingdom of God come upon you" (Matt. 12:28). Our enemy is too subtle and dangerous for us, but the Body of Christ not only provides for us; it covers us. We can all put on Christ as our armor. Against him Satan's shafts are of no avail!

It is the Church that overcomes. Spiritual warfare is the task of the Church, not of the individual. We take Ephesians 6 for ourselves individually—and I do not say there is *no* individual application of the armor—but the individual by himself cannot "put on *the whole* armor of God" any more than he can comprehend alone the measure of the love of Christ. Seen in the light of the rest of Ephesians, it is, I feel sure, armor for *the Body*—a special piece for each member. For to try and fight this warfare alone is to invite trouble from an enemy who has no fear of the individual, but who dreads the one Body. Without the protection of the whole armor, he will single us out. Under its shadow he cannot touch us.

This explains why, faced with a true spiritual issue in the realm of the heavenly warfare, we shall always find ourselves driven *together* to pray it through, even if it be with only one other member. The Lord cannot use heroes, but praise God, he can make great use of weak members of the Body!

THE FULLNESS OF HIM

As we close these chapters on the Church, I want us to pause and put to ourselves a question.

Some of us are serving the Lord in mission fields, others at home, and we praise him for his calling wherever it may be. But let us ask ourselves now, Is our ministry purely that of evangelism as a thing sufficient in itself, or is it bound up with something altogether larger? Having glimpsed the full thought of God as it is revealed especially through Paul, is it possible that we could be content to stop short at the business of bringing souls to the Lord, and not be deeply concerned also for the greater purpose into which those souls are being brought?

Dear brothers and sisters, this is a great challenge. I know many feel that to be evangelical and to win souls is all that God requires of us in these last days; but is it so? We bless God for Peter's primary ministry, without which the House of God will have no "living stones." We long to see men saved from perishing and won for his glory. What is more, God has not only given to his Church "some evangelists" for this task, but surely too he says to every one of us, "Do the work of an evangelist" (Eph. 4:11; 2 Tim. 4:5).

But, do we stop there? When we see three or four thousand converts, all saved and all going on fairly well spiritually, do we feel a task has been accomplished? Should we not regard it rather as a task just begun? Ought we not to ask ourselves how many of those three or four thousand have yet caught a glimpse of the one heavenly Man into which God has brought them? Are they still just units, fishes in the net, figures in a list of "campaign results," or does that supreme vision possess them? It will certainly not do so unless it first possesses us. So I ask again, Are we burdened, as were the apostles, to see them grow up in all things into the Head, even Christ?

I am well aware that this question has implications that are far from easy. To face them may well bring some of us into collision with ideas and traditions from which such high thoughts have long been left out of account. A great deal of our work may have to be re-evaluated. Many "heads" may have to be chopped off, many minds readjusted, many human authorities—our own included—made to give way to the Headship of the One.

I confess I would like nevertheless to plead with you—yea, if I could, to persuade you—to press on at any cost into the full thought of God. But persuasion and entreaty are useless if we do not see what God has in mind—and by that I do not mean see the reasonableness of it. If we only see its reasonableness, we shall have very often to remind ourselves how it was we arrived at that conclusion, or we shall very soon be as easily swayed back again. But if once we have seen God's new Man in Christ, a heavenly reality is opened to us, and things will never be quite the same again. Many a time reason would say, "It may be well enough in some parts of the world, but in my situation here, things are difficult, nay, impossible. I see no hope of realizing what I see in the Word, so let me be content with simpler things." But oh, my friends, while we may never underrate the blessed ministry of the net that

brings men in, let us seek grace to follow on with
Paul to the vision of the Body, the earthly tabernacle where God would dwell amid his own and
manifest his fullness today.

For the Church, he tells us, is "the fullness of
him that filleth all in all." She is the vessel to
contain and express his wisdom, life and power.
Such fullness cannot be known individually. The
apostle is emphatic about this. It is together that
we become a habitation of God through the
Spirit. It is through the Church that the wisdom
of God is manifested to spiritual powers. It is
with all saints that we receive the full knowledge
of divine love. It is as the Body of Christ that we
attain to the full grown Man. It is clad in the
whole armor that we withstand in the evil day.
(Eph. 1:23; 2:22; 3:10, 18, 19; 4:13; 6:11.) Every
analogy he uses in Ephesians reinforces his argument that the Church, not the individual, is
the vessel of fullness.

Because God's children today do not function
together as the Body, they have become as a leak-
ing vessel. Shatter a glass tumbler and what
happens? Each piece may perhaps hold a little
water, but it is as nothing compared to what the
unbroken tumbler held. So is it in spiritual
things. The individual receives in but two dimensions, as it were; the Church in three. Ten
thousand Christians are one thing; ten thousand
members of the Body are quite another.

Revelation is perfect only when it is revelation
to the whole Church. Today the Head has much
more to give, but the Body is a leaky vessel, unable to contain it. It is quite true that individuals

do make some progress in many points of the faith—but merely as individuals; they do not, as such, advance one inch in the stature of the fullness of Christ. There must be a return to the one vessel. Not to believing the same doctrine, nor to using the same methods, nor even to having fellowship with all: none of these is enough. We must see ourselves in the same Body, one in Christ Jesus. Let us ask the Lord to illumine our hearts.

10
John –and the Truth

As he approached the end of his life, Paul wrote a letter to his young fellow worker Timothy. Tragically, we may feel, this last-preserved of the apostle's writings has as its burden the sad fact of spiritual declension and departure. Yet it is just because that spiritual departure had set in even before the death of the apostles that there is found within the pages of the New Testament guidance for the saints under the circumstances today.

In an hour when many are losing their faith

and hope, and are lowering their Christian standards, it is easy to become confused. We are tempted to say, If the faith of God's children can so change, is there anything that cannot? True, the Lord himself never changes; but while we can look up and praise him, nevertheless we look around and are troubled. So the Spirit through Paul shows us something else that is unchanging. "The firm foundation of God standeth, having this seal, The Lord knoweth them that are his: and, Let every one that nameth the name of the Lord depart from unrighteousness" (2 Tim. 2:19).

Men may go; Phygelus and Hermogenes, Hymenaeus and Philetus, yes, all Asia too, may prove unfaithful to the Lord; and when one by one they do, we begin to look around and wonder who at all is to be counted upon. But *the Lord knows* them that are his: that is the first seal inscribed upon this sure foundation. We may be mistaken; God never is. We need to confess before him that we may estimate wrongly, but that he sees into all hearts. We overrate men because God in mercy uses them; but he has used us too, and yet, God knows, we need his mercy! Let us beware of thinking we know human nature. Only God has that knowledge. Men may disappoint, but have we not all of us at some time failed the Lord?

So there is a second element in this seal or inscription, a command laid upon all who would "call upon the Lord out of a pure heart." They who name his Name are to *depart from unrighteousness.* The unshakeable foundation of God tells us this. When we see spiritual breakdown around us, we are to look to ourselves. For they who are the Lord's are to be sanctified men. The verses immediately following elaborate this. They speak of a great house with its furnishings, vessels of gold and silver, wood and earth, suitable to various tasks. Men are likened to such vessels, but are urged to qualify themselves for places of honor there.

What is this "great house" with its vessels destined to honor or dishonor, and the implication of moral qualities behind those words? In 1 Timothy the Church of God *is* the house of God (3:15); but here I believe Paul has in view not that, but the outward profession of Christianity. The "Church of the living God" could never itself be a ruin; it could never degenerate into this "great house" with its element of mixture. But the Church's outward testimony may, alas, at any particular time be in ruins.

What now distinguishes between these vessels? We note at once that only their materials are specified, not their function. Clearly, in keeping with the construction of the house which we considered earlier, here again it is not relative usefulness but quality of materials that counts. Gold and silver vessels are less practically useful than wooden furniture or earthenware pots, but God is not here discussing with us what they will be used for; he is judging their lasting value to himself. In a day of declension God looks beyond mere usefulness to intrinsic worth, and a few ounces of gold may equal in value a whole hall full of wooden benches! In spiritual terms, two different men may utter almost identical words, but the power lies not merely in what they say but in who they are. Balaam and Isaiah both spoke of the Kingdom, but we know well to which of the two we would turn in personal need.

What do we prize in a day when values are slipping: the wood and the earth of human cleverness and wordly resources, or the gold and the silver of divine origin and redemption through the Cross? Many things in Christianity have become too cheap today, but there is no easy shortcut to spiritual worth. Preaching, prayer, witness, these may not seem difficult, but to be of value they will be costly in years and blood and the discipline of God's dealings. The "vessel unto honor" is the man who has waited for the Spirit to teach him, and who has not been ashamed meanwhile to admit he does not know. For there comes a day when the true character of things is tested. Preaching, in an hour of departure and confusion, is of little value unless men see God in it. At such a time they can tell whether the speaker has really been taken by God through the things of which he speaks. What has not already touched him deeply will have little power to touch others in that day.

Though the very idea of a "vessel" suggests formation for something, 2 Timothy hints at circumstances in which we should do well to leave to God the destiny of the vessels, and to concern ourselves above all with their quality. "If a man therefore purge himself from these, he shall be a vessel unto honor."

HIS SERVANT JOHN

This brings us at length to the beloved disciple. In point of time his writings fall, in general, after those of Paul, and in keeping with this, his most distinctive contribution to the New Testament revelation is, as we have said, just this very emphasis upon recovery. At a time when the Church was taken up with outward things at the expense of the inward life, John came on the scene to remind men of the true divine qualities. This, we suggested earlier, is illustrated for us at the outset by the account of Jesus discovering him and his brother James "in the boat mending their nets"—making good, that is, damage occasioned by the previous night's toil.

John, of course, was no less a "fisherman" in the full sense than was Peter, and equally it would seem that, within his sphere, he was no less a "builder" than was Paul. We find him at the beginning of the Acts sharing fully in the preaching and fellowship of the early phases, and like Paul he too can write authoritatively "to the church" (3 John 9). But seen in the context of the New Testament as a whole, the feature of John's writings that stands out most prominently is surely this particular ministry of recalling things to their original or divinely intended state.

As we all know, John's is the last of the four Gospels. His Epistles too are the last epistles; and his Revelation is placed last in the whole Book of God. All his writings are in some sense "the last." In John's Gospel you find everywhere the reflection of this fact. John touches on very little of the work of the Lord as it is set forth, for example, in Mark. Neither does he concern himself with the commandments of the Lord as they are dealt with by Matthew in the Sermon on the Mount. He is not so troubled about what you should do if someone takes away your coat, or whether, when pressed by your neighbor, you should go with him one mile or two. That is not his first concern now. His burden relates to the life of the eternities and to your right relation thereto. If you go back to that, he implies, everything else will follow. In this he is quite different, too, from Luke. He is not occupied with outward and temporal things—with dates and genealogies, even though they take you right back to Adam. His whole burden is this, that we must get right behind these various things to *the Life.* Everything here now is in disrepair. Go back to the Life that "came down from heaven," and when you get back there, Peter and all that he stands for will be preserved, and so will Paul. In a sense, John has nothing new to offer. He does not take us further, for the furthest point has already been touched by God. The purpose of the revelation entrusted to John is to bring back people again to that original purpose, by bringing them into a fresh touch with the risen Lord of life himself.

Reading through the Gospel of John you cannot but be impressed with the fact that the first chapter is the key to all that follows. In that first chapter you find grace and truth, the two streams flowing from Christ. "The law was given by

Moses; grace and truth came by Jesus Christ"
(1:17). Throughout the Gospel you find the same
double emphasis, upon truth on the one hand
and upon grace on the other. Truth will always
make demands, and grace will always be there to
meet them. In the incident recorded in Chapter 8
of the woman taken in adultery, truth shines
forth. Jesus did not say to her, "It is all right; you
have not sinned." He did not tell the Jews that
what she had done was nothing serious, and that
he was not deeply concerned about it. No, the
Lord said: "He that is without sin among you, let
him first cast a stone at her" (8:7). The truth was
there: "She has sinned, and according to the law
she ought to be stoned"; but so also was the
grace, for when all had gone out, he turned and
said to her: "Neither do I condemn thee."
Throughout the Gospel of John you will find
truth is always matched by grace in this way.

When however you turn to the Epistles of John,
you find something more. You hear less of grace
and truth as such, for these letters are written at a
later date, and an even more fundamental recovery is necessary. You therefore find John pointing you further back still. "God is light" (1 John
1:5). "God is love" (1 John 4:8). Whereas, in the
Gospel, Christ coming from the Father was revealed among men as grace and truth, here in the
Epistles, Christ in existence with the Father is
revealed to men as light and love. What has been
truth in the Gospel becomes light in the Epistles.
What has been grace in the Gospel becomes love
in the Epistles. Why is this? Because that which
is light in God, when transmitted to men, be-

comes truth; that which is love in God, when brought to men, becomes grace. Love goes back to God, but grace stays here. Everything that is in God is light and love, but coming out to men it becomes truth and grace. And it is always possible for grace to be misused, truth to be mishandled; men have misappropriated these things to themselves. But God is light and God is love, and you cannot climb up there and touch that; that is beyond mishandling. So John's method is to take us right back there to the Throne, not to offer us something novel, but to confront us again with the original. It is by going back again to the Source that we shall recover and preserve what has been lost.

But it is when we come to the last, and in some ways the most important, book in the whole Bible, the Book of the Revelation, that we see this principle of the apostle's brought fully into play, and I think we shall find that his emphasis here is especially upon the Lord Jesus as "he that is true" (Rev. 3:7). I think none of us could read that book without realizing that it represents the supreme restoration. It marks the complete reversal of Genesis. Everything of failure and breakdown that entered in at the beginning is now undone; everything that was lost is recovered; every question raised there is answered here.

In Genesis I see a serpent. What is going to be the end of this? I see a curse. What is going to be the end of that? I see death and sin. Where will that end? I see man barred from the Tree of life. What will be the issue of these things? I see their beginnings, but what is their end? And what is going to be the end of me? God in grace has made a beginning with me, but what if salvation were to end with the present? The purpose of the Book of Revelation is to answer these questions by introducing me to Jesus as alive for evermore, the Beginning *and* the End.

For the Revelation is the unveiling, the *apokalypsis*, of Jesus Christ. It draws aside the curtain and reveals his Person. Its object is not primarily to enlighten us regarding coming events—the antichrist, the supposed revival of the Roman empire, the rapture, the millennium, or the ultimate destiny of Satan. John's remedy for our ills is not a matter of so many seals and so many trumpets, nor is it an answer to the question whether the rapture is "partial" or "complete." It is not in fact designed to satisfy our intellectual speculations at all, but to meet our spiritual need by revealing Christ himself in fullness, that we may know *him*.

True, the Revelation does answer our questions as to ourselves, and in ways surpassing even our dreams. For what John presents to us at the end is in fact more than we lost at the beginning. God began with a garden and he ends with a city. In Genesis he visited the man whom he had made; in Revelation his dwelling place, nay, his very throne, is in the midst of men. For what had been the Church in Paul has become the Holy City in John. Yet in the divine intention this was always so. For what God had set himself to do at the first, he will indeed do; and Revelation assures us that, in his own mind, he has already done it. So in essence John presents us, as before, with nothing new; he only shows us that what God intended he will carry into effect.

All this John does, I repeat, by bringing us back to the divine Original. What is the destiny of this world? What is to be the outcome of the Church's conflict? What will be the end of me? Everything, John affirms, has its answer and its fulfillment in the Lord Jesus Christ. Is Christ my Beginning? He is also my End. Is he my Alpha? He is also my Omega. Christ is the answer to all my questions. If I am clear first about him, I shall know all I need to know about coming events—the reason for them and the rightness of them. But that is the inescapable divine order. No one is qualified to study the subsequent visions recorded by John who has not seen that first vision of the Lord himself. For that tells us who he is, even the risen and victorious King of kings, and the events that follow are the outcome of his being that.

This was true for John personally. Even the beloved disciple who had lain on Jesus' bosom must have a revelation of his eternal Lord that shattered him in the dust. Only after that might he be shown "things to come." The first seeing is fundamental to all other seeing. For what is in view is a kingdom; and it is the King and his subjects, not the experts in prophecy, who proclaim war on all that is contrary to his kingdom. Coming events are not revealed to provide food for idle speculation; their goal is the overthrow of the enemy and the universal reign of the Christ.

So in the Revelation, God shows us an aspect of his Son not shown to us in the Gospels. In the Gospels we see him as Savior, in Revelation as King; in John's Gospel as Alpha, in Revelation as Omega. The one displays his love, the other his majesty. In the upper room Jesus girds himself about the waist, for service; at Patmos he is discovered girt about the breasts, for war. In the Gospels his mild eyes melted Peter; in Revelation they are as a flame of fire. There his voice was gentle, calling his own sheep by name, and gracious words proceeded out of his mouth; here his voice is terrible as the sound of many waters, and from his mouth there proceeds a sharp two-edged sword, striking death to his foes.

It is not enough that we know Jesus as Lamb of God and as Savior of the world; we must know him also as God's Christ, God's King; God's Judge. When we see him as Savior, we say, "How lovable!" and lean on his bosom. When we see him as Monarch we say, "How terrible!" and fall prostrate at his feet. The one issues in thanksgiving, the other in worship. To see him now as King is, one might almost say, to see "another" Christ, to experience "another" salvation. We behold him now as the faithful and true Witness, the divine Guarantor that, though the purposes of God may perhaps be hindered, they can never be finally thwarted.

HE THAT IS TRUE

In studying the Apocalypse, we need to be careful to avoid overspiritualizing what we read.

John's new heaven and new earth are real, not imaginary, and his new Jerusalem is real, just as truly as the risen Lord is real. The spiritualizing away of divine things is the desperate expedient of people who do not possess the reality. Many dear folk amass spiritual and prophetic truth only, I fear, to build for themselves with it an unreal world. To do this is to escape from reality, just as truly as do those who, as we saw earlier, are ready enough today to live in the spiritual atmosphere of Ephesians but want to avoid facing the practical challenge of 1 Corinthians. But remember, this was the very delusion that overtook Laodicea, making it possible for them to believe a lie.

The mark of spiritual maturity will always be that divine things become real to us because Christ is real to us. We see him as real life, real holiness—as "the truth," in fact; and I use "truth" here in a sense very different from my use of it above when speaking of "prophetic truth." Many confuse truth and doctrine, but the two are not the same. Doctrine is what is said on earth about the eternal truth. I know well that our word truth in Chinese is *chen-li* (roughly, "reality-doctrine") but the Greek meaning is in fact *chen* without the *li*, "reality" without the "doctrine." The Jesus who said, "Ye shall know the truth" (John 8:32) himself embodies all that is true (Rev. 3:7; cf. 1 John 5:20), and it is thus that we should know him.

Truth "is in Jesus" (Eph. 4:21), and, like grace, it "came through Jesus Christ" (John 1:17). We welcome his grace; but do we know his truth?

Grace came to us in an historical act when he gave himself upon the Cross; but no less certainly is truth intimately bound up with his Person and work, and not merely something expressed through his preaching. Thus if grace extends to us now, truth should just as surely extend to and embrace us who, through faith in that finished work, are now found united with him.

Yet while many know him as the Way and the Life, too few in fact know him today as the Truth. This is a serious deficiency, for truth, we said, is reality. Before him and apart from him there is no reality. And we can enter into the truth, if we will, because his finished work remains for us today the truest thing in the world. What we are before God, we are *in reality* because of what he has done.

This has an important bearing on our practical experience. My theoretical difficulty is always this, that what I am before God, when compared with what I am here, reveals all too frequently that much is wrong. What Christ's work has made me is one thing, but what I experience on earth far too often appears to contradict the truth of that. How do I make good the discrepancy? How do I live so that my conduct here expresses consistently what I know to be true there?

What I have to see is that what, through the work of Christ, God has made me to be in him *is the real thing*. And it is the foundation of all my true Christian experience. Nothing else is. What I have become by virtue of being in Christ is the eternal truth. My one fault will be to dwell in my feelings and experiences, my strivings and failures, my misgivings and hopes, and not to fix my faith upon "him that is true."

Everything centers in him. At the very heart of Scripture we see Christ on the Cross. In his death we were included, and when he arose we arose with him, members of his Body. John reveals him to us as he is today, and, praise God, his ascension and glory are ours! But whence do we derive our certainty of these things? Not from our feelings, but from the reality of his Person and his work. What Christ has done is the resting place of our faith. It is not our feelings, nor even our knowledge, that "makes us free." It is the truth. What John 8:32 shows us is that, until we see these things, we remain enslaved, but that because Christ's work is real, and because what we have become in him is the truth, the mere discovery of these realities opens the way for them, by their very nature, to bring to an end our bondage.

This is the great value to us of John's new unveiling of Jesus. Viewed from a merely human level—from the standpoint, for example, of a Roman prisoner in the isle called Patmos—Christ's victory is more unlike reality than almost anything we can think of. That was so then, and it is so today. We look at governments, society, outward Christianity, and see bondage, oppression, frustration—anything but liberty. So we pray and ask for victory, and in doing so give the lie to the victory of Calvary. The truth, the glorious reality, is that Christ has already conquered, not that he is going to. What God does today is something already *done* in Christ. Our extreme need is to see that fact.

"O send out thy light and thy truth" (Psalm 43:3). The two are connected. The truth is complete in Christ, but the need of our hearts is to have God's light shed on it. All spiritual experience comes from divine light on eternal truth. Truth preached without light becomes doctrine; with divine light it becomes revelation. It always comes to us as one or the other. But the Truth, the eternal reality, is Christ himself, and then, what God by his grace has made us to be in him.

CHRIST AND TIME

Spiritual reality has this outstanding characteristic, that it bears no mark of time. The time factor vanishes the instant you touch that reality. Take, for example, prophecy. From the human point of view there is such a thing as prophecy, but from the divine point of view no such thing exists. True, we read, "Thou art my Son, this day have I begotten thee," but with God "this day" is always. Our Lord says he is the First and the Last, the Alpha and the Omega; but remember, he is both together, both at once. It is not that at one time he is First and at another time he is Last; he is First and Last simultaneously. Nor is it that having for a while been Alpha he later on becomes Omega; he is Alpha and Omega from eternity to eternity. He is always First *and* Last; he is always Alpha *and* Omega. Of course, in the sight of men he is not Omega until he is manifested as Omega, but in the sight of God he is Omega now. With man, past and future are separate and distinct; with God they synchronize. With me the "I" of yesterday differs from the "I" of today, and the "I" of tomorrow differs still further; but Jesus Christ is the same yesterday and today and forever. He is the eternal "I AM."

It is here that the knowledge of God becomes so precious to us. Our Lord said to Nicodemus, "No man hath ascended into heaven, but he that descended out of heaven, even the Son of man, which is in heaven" (John 3:13). You note how these two positions synchronize in Christ. There is no change of time or place with him. He is at once there and here. So of God it is written that he is "the Father of lights, with whom can be no variation, neither shadow that is cast by turning" (James 1:17). He is that in himself; he is that in his Christ; and praise his Name, he is that, too, in his Church!

Have you ever come across the Church that Paul describes in Ephesians 1:18 in terms of "the riches of the glory of his inheritance in the saints"? Or that depicted in 1 Corinthians 6:11 as "washed ... sanctified ... justified in the name of the Lord Jesus, and in the Spirit of our God"? Oh, you say, that describes the *position* of the Church. No, it describes the *reality* of the Church. In writing to the Romans, Paul was more daring than were some of his translators. He wrote "called saints," or "saints by calling," but they felt it was running too great a risk to translate literally, so they safeguarded their conception of spiritual things by writing "called *to be* saints" (1:7). If we are only called "to be" saints, how long shall we have to be "being" before we can actually *be?* Praise God, we *are* saints!

The expression translated "We are his workmanship" (Eph. 2:10) could as well be rendered: "We are his masterpiece." The Church is the very best God can produce. It can never be improved upon. We look around and see breakdown everywhere, and we wonder, "What is the Church coming to?" I tell you, she is not "coming to" anything; she has arrived. We do not look forward to discover her goal; we look back. God reached his end in Christ before the foundation of the world, and we move forward with him on the basis of what already is. As we move in the light of that eternal fact, we witness its progressive manifestation.

Christian progress is not a question of attaining to some abstract standard, or of pressing through to some far-off goal. It is wholly a question of seeing God's standard. You advance spiritually by finding out what you really are, not by trying to become what you hope to be. That goal you will never reach, however earnestly you strive. It is when you *see* you are dead that you die; it is when you *see* you are risen that you arise; it is when you *see* you are holy that you become holy. Seeing the accomplished fact determines the pathway to the realizing of that fact. The end is reached by seeing, not by desiring or working. The only possibility of spiritual progress lies in our discovering the truth as God sees it; the truth concerning Christ, the truth concerning ourselves in Christ, and the truth concerning the Church, the Body of Christ.

In Romans 8:30 Paul tells us that those whom God has foreordained he has called, that those whom he has called he has justified, and that those whom he has justified he has glorified. Thus, according to God's Word, all who are called have already been glorified. The goal is attained. The Church has already come to glory!

"Oh, but this is too difficult!" you exclaim. "Surely the Church must need cleansing! Please come back to Ephesians 5, and tell me again how you explain the statement that the Church is cleansed by the washing of water with the word?" Very well, but kindly first observe the context. It tells us how a husband and wife should act. Love is required of the husband, and submission of the wife. The question is not how to be a husband or how to be a wife, but how, being a husband or a wife, you should live. It is not that you must love in order to be a husband or that you must obey in order to be a wife, but that, being a husband you should love, being a wife you should obey. The whole point at issue is not of doing in order to be at all, but of doing because of being.

Now does not the same principle apply in regard to the Church? The called-out ones are not washed in order to be the Church; they are washed because they are the Church. That is why I suggested earlier that Paul here is looking beyond the question of sin. The object of washing may be refreshment by removal of the tarnish and dust of the world, in the sense implied in the Lord's words in John 13:10. And that is, I think, what is intended here. The Church *has been washed* (1 Cor. 6:11), so by washing she is now kept fresh. The husband acts as a husband because he is a husband; the wife acts as a wife because she is a wife; the Church is washed because she has been washed. The Church has reached the standard, so she is helped to live in accord with the standard, whereas that which is not the Church could never become the Church by any amount of washing.

As we stated in an earlier chapter, whereas Romans arrives at the statement "them he also glorified" (8:30) by working through the whole story of redemption, Ephesians deliberately goes outside of time into eternity past and future, and takes the eternal fullness as its starting-point. For the ultimate reality is always before God, and God speaks of his Church in the light of that reality. The time factor in the Bible is one of the greatest problems to the human mind, but it vanishes from the horizon when once our hearts have been enlightened to know the glory of his inheritance in the saints. God sees the Church utterly pure, utterly perfect. To know today the ultimate glory in heaven is the one sure way of living in the power of that glory on earth.

CITIZENS OF HEAVEN

It remains a sad fact, but a true one, that many Christians have only seen the outward form of Christianity. They have never seen the inward reality, and so as yet have no knowledge of its essential nature. And no wonder, for today so much that is merely external has become attached to Christianity that it is difficult to discern what is truly of God. Yet Christianity is not, after all, merely a system of externals. It is "the Truth."

The Gospel of John comes to our help here by presenting to us the Holy Spirit as the Spirit of truth, and assures us that he will lead us into all the Truth. We shall have something more to say of this in our concluding chapter. But surely we may deduce from this statement that what comes to us apart from the Holy Spirit's instruction and enlightenment is something less than the Truth. What we can arrive at by thought and study, by the seeing of the eye and the hearing of the ear, is all outside the realm of eternal verity; it is not spiritually real.

The human mind has adopted some wide extremes of view on divine things. The Church of Rome, for example, has sought to give them a sacramental or materialistic explanation. Men have fixed their gaze on the material water of baptism and credited it with regenerative power. The material elements of the Lord's supper are likewise said to be miraculously transformed into the physical body and blood of Christ, providing us with the well-known doctrine of transubstantiation. And in keeping with these ideas, the outward form of the Church, as Rome understands that outward form, is held by her to be the one true Church. At the opposite extreme the intellectual man, puzzled by the evident inconsistencies resulting from such a view, has sought to remove them or explain them away by developing what we may call the Reformed view of things. He distinguishes between the outward ceremony of baptism and the inward reality. He sees the elements of the Supper as symbols that are merely representative and typical. And he solves the problem of the Church by arguing for a true and a false, a heavenly and an earthly, and a so-called "Church within the Church."

I ask you, does either of these extremes do real justice to the plain statements of Scripture? The Word says nothing of true and false, or of representation or symbolism, but makes only firm statements of fact. "We are buried therefore with him through baptism into death," says Paul (Rom. 6:4; Col. 2:12). To him there is no such thing as a baptism not involving a dying and rising with Christ. He had no thought that a Christian could experience baptism on a certain date, and at a later date enter into the experience of death and resurrection with Christ. Similarly our Lord's words concerning the cup. "This is my blood," go far beyond mere symbolism on the one hand, while on the other, his allusion to it almost in the same breath as "the fruit of the vine" equally disposes of the idea of transubstantiation. It is his blood, but it is also still a cup of wine. There is not here the "representative" and the "real," the type and the antitype, but only one divine reality.

We need anointed eyes to see. We can only be brought to the truth of baptism and the Lord's supper by the Spirit of truth. When we have been, there will cease to be a "doctrine" of these things; there will be reality alone. We may speak words that to extreme Reformists sound alarmingly like the words Rome speaks, but we shall be seeing what Rome never saw. For to those who have seen the Ultimate, the doctrine and type both give way to that vision of him. There is only the Truth.

But what we have just said about the reality of Baptism and the Lord's table is no less true when we come to speak of the reality of the Church. Nowadays, at the very mention of the word "Church," many evangelical Christians become quite apprehensive. Whenever the subject is brought up, great precautions are taken to clear the ground lest any confusion arise in the minds of the hearers. Care is exercised to differentiate between the true Church and the false. But in the Lord's Word, and in the thought of God, there is no such distinction. The Lord put no footnote in Scripture when he spoke of the Church. He did not seek to safeguard the spiritual reality by differentiating between an inward and an outward, a real and an unreal. He did not even draw a clear line of demarcation between the local and the universal. In the Word of God there is only "the Church."

Notwithstanding this, the subject of the Church continues to be widely regarded as a controversial one, to be studiously avoided for the sake of evangelical unity. At a great convention in England I asked a worker, "Why at this convention does one hear no mention of the Church?" "Oh," he replied, "because this convention is for the deepening of the spiritual life."

So, if his view was a representative one, the Church and the spiritual life of the Christian are thought by many to be unrelated, whereas nothing is more intimately related to the spiritual life of the children of God than is the Church.

"Oh to be like Thee!" is a hymn which the individual may sing, but not the Church, for the Church *is* the heavenly Body of Christ. To discover this is to have one's Christian life revolutionized. For though most Christians admit that to struggle and strive after heavenliness is wrong, yet still they struggle and strive. They have been taught to regard heavenliness as something to be attained, and so, for them, Christianity is an endeavor to be what they are not and to do what they cannot do. They struggle not to love the world because in fact, at heart, they really love it; they strive to be humble because, at heart, they are so self-assured. This is the experience of so-called Christianity, but, I repeat, it is not the experience of the Church. For though we may work our way across the Atlantic or the Pacific, we can never work our way from earth to heaven. Heaven is not a place that the Church will reach at some future date. The Church *is* there, and never was anywhere else.

Heaven is both the origin and the abode of the Church, but not her destination. And since the Church has never known any other sphere but heaven, the question of striving to reach heaven can never arise for her. This may seem a drastic statement, but it is a fact. Like everything else in the Word of God, it is something to be seen by the Holy Spirit's revelation to our hearts; and not till we see it do we know our heavenly calling. That calling does not call us into heaven, but makes known to us that we are of heaven and in heaven. So the Church is not a company of Christians working their way heavenward, but a company who are actually now citizens of heaven. Remember again: "No man hath ascended into heaven, but ... the Son of man, which is in heaven." The Church need not pray that she may become like Christ. She needs only to see her place there in union with her Lord.

We need to revise our thinking about the Church. It is not an organization to be planned, nor is it just a company of people to be completed. It is not a concept to be grasped, nor an ideal to be attained. Like so much else that is ours in Christ, the Church is a reality to be seen with the help of the Holy Spirit through the Word. When we recognize the real heavenly character of the Church, then the heavenliness of our own renewed nature dawns upon us, and we *know* that our starting-point as Christians is not earth but heaven. The Church is perfect, perfect beyond any possibility of improvement. Theologians say: "Oh, but that is the standing of the Church; her state is not so." But in the sight of God there is no imperfection in the Church eternally. Why be bothered with the endless questions that relate to the old creation? They simply vanish when, by divine grace, we see the eternal reality. The Church is the sphere in which God exercises his authority in the earth, and today, in the midst of a polluted universe, he has a sphere of unsullied purity for his own abode.

GOLDEN LAMPSTANDS

How nervous we are about the Church! How reluctant to trust ourselves to her! We say: What if the Church should make a mistake? What if she should come to the wrong conclusion? But the Lord made no provision for failure of any kind there. It is as though, in his thought, no such contingency could arise. We think of the Church in Corinth as a church far below standard, but it was to that church that Paul wrote: "Ye were washed ... ye were sanctified ... ye were justified." Even in Rome at the end, he does not see Demas and Alexander the coppersmith and a host of false brethren constituting some kind of false church, to be carefully distinguished from the real. Whenever in his epistles Paul mentions the Church, he speaks of her as altogether perfect, and he inserts no modifying clauses for the sake of avoiding misapprehension.

With John it is no different. In Revelation 2 and 3 we are shown the Son of man moving among the lampstands, and affirming the individual responsibility of each to himself. Our eyes, following his, readily detect the many failures in the churches; but has it occurred to us that John nowhere distinguishes between the churches that are right and the churches that are wrong? For all their faultiness, he writes of them as the Lord himself still sees them, namely, as "seven golden lampstands," seven candlesticks *all of gold*.

To those upon whom divine reality has once begun to dawn there is only that reality. We say:

From God's point of view the Church ought to be this or that. No, the Church *is* this or that! The Church is what from God's point of view it ought to be, because Christ is that. To see eternal reality in Christ is to cease to differentiate between what the Church is potentially and actually. And once the Lord has begun to open our eyes, we no longer despise small things. We no longer say, when we meet only a handful of believers in some place, "Of what use is this to God? There are so few here!" We do not complain, "There is only one other brother with me in this pagan city!" We look at the Acts, and we cease to be distressed at the fewness of the believers who in Chapter 13 took such far-reaching decisions (for that is what they indeed proved to be). We cease to think: There was an inadequate representation of the Church there; such important steps as these ought to have awaited a general council of the Church's leaders.

No, we are satisfied that those believers saw the heavenly reality, and hence were not unduly bothered about niceties of technique. And when we see the reality of the Church as they saw it, then we shall recognize the Church in operation when we encounter it anywhere, be it even in a small group of believers with, as men would say, no special standing as its "duly appointed representatives." If they themselves are truly subject to the Head in all things, and if they are making much, not of themselves or the Church, but of Christ, then the Spirit of God will always bear witness to them.

Take an extreme case. When in Damascus

Ananias went to Saul, he went alone, and alone he laid hands on Saul. "Out of order!" you exclaim. "Quite contrary to the principles of the Body! Surely that was independent action!" Not at all! Ananias was just a disciple, it is true, but one moving (as a member of the Body should) under the direction of the Head. And in that hour the Lord's eyes were not on Ananias alone, but also on the other man. It was the very action of Ananias towards this new brother that expressed so clearly his own subjection to Christ; and under these conditions, when he moved, the whole Body moved.

If you have been brought into the eternal reality of the Church, the day may well come when you yourself are called to speak and act for the whole Church. Will you refuse to do so then? A movement on the part of any one member of the Body who is truly subject to the Spirit of Christ is a movement of the whole. The life of such a one in that hour transcends all externalities, for men recognize that God is moving through that member.

The implications of all this are very great. We have no business to view things materialistically or intellectually—that is, through the eyes of Rome or of the Reformation—but only from the standpoint of God. God sees "seven golden lampstands." He knows only "the Church," and when we permit the Spirit of truth to lead us into the spiritual truth of the Church, we shall see only the Church that God sees.

As I speak of these things to Christians in various countries. I find that they all, leaders included, have the same questions. "Do you mean to tell me," they exclaim, "that it is possible to have something according to God *down here*? You are an idealist. You are following a mirage. But even supposing you are right, and it is possible to see these things come to pass in some measure in your lifetime, what about the next generation? What you are experiencing now will go the way of everything else. Its character will change, and within a few years it will survive only as a caricature of your vision."[1]

Yes, I suppose if you look at things only from the standpoint of the ministry of Paul in the New Testament, such an attitude may appear a right one: but thank God, there is still the ministry of John. What God was doing through these men is eternal—not just something for ten or twenty years. There is no "first generation" and "second generation" about God's spiritual house.[2] It is "from generation to generation." What God has in view he will never abandon, for the very good reason that he himself never changes. Dare we then accept another standard? A person who cannot afford to wear pearls buys a string of

[1]It may be well at this point to remind readers that, for the past thirty-five years, the author has witnessed the growth, through the preaching of the Word, of a most fruitful work of the Spirit of God in China, and one that, through the power of Christ indwelling his own, has weathered the severest storms.—Ed.

[2]The allusion, of course, is to the difference between first and second generation Christians—between those delivered to Christ from paganism on the first wave of an evangelical missionary movement, and those who so often grow up after them as Christians only in name.—Ed.

paste beads and thinks of them as imitation pearls. But the one who can afford to wear pearls does not think of the paste beads even as imitation pearls. To her there are not real pearls and false pearls; there are only pearls. The paste beads have for her no more connection with pearls than have any other beads; the only pearls she recognizes as pearls at all are real pearls.

"And having turned I saw seven golden candlesticks." "And he carried me away in the Spirit to a mountain great and high, and showed me the holy city Jerusalem, coming down out of heaven from God, having the glory of God: her light was like unto a stone most precious...." Keeping our eyes there, we can praise God for the ministry of John!

11
He That Overcometh

John the apostle reaffirms that God's end is certain, and that his ways now are consistent with that end. Just as, in the heavenly City at the last, the principles of the Body find their fullest development and expression, so is the reverse also true. Whenever the life of the eternities has a free course in us today, we shall find every feature of the heavenly City, every true character of the Lord Jesus, manifesting itself through his Body here on the earth. And who that has once caught a glimpse of God's heavenly Man can ever be satisfied with anything less than this?

But now we must be practical, and take a look at conditions around us. Most of us will agree that outward Christianity today is in a sorry state. It manifests all the ailments and weaknesses of the world. Its work is reduced to a little preaching and a little social service. Its impact on men is negligible. This is a fact; but what should cause us even greater personal distress is the tragedy that, as God's people, our conscience has been so little exercised about this fact. We take things as a matter of course, and many seem indeed to accept them almost as though they ought to be as they are. Christians today do not believe that what Paul has set before us is possible. Such unbelief should have the effect of driving us back to the ministry of John, and compelling us to look again at its special character.

What the Lord revealed through Paul concerning the Body of Christ was intended, as we saw earlier, to be realized in local churches each expressing that Body. In different localities there would be a true practical expression, not of a host of different bodies, but of one Body. This was the divine intention, and this was how things began. But we know how sadly they failed, and how the Lord himself had to speak again from heaven. In doing so he touched a new note concerning the Church and the churches, and this is why the second and third chapters of Revelation are so helpful. In those chapters, the Lord Jesus uses John to bring to light a further divine provision for his Church. I refer to the seven promises at the ends of those seven letters.

In them we have John's special message for a time of general departure. It is that, amid conditions of decay and general ruin, God looks for those of his people who will be his overcomers within the churches.

What is the meaning of an "overcomer"? To avoid misunderstanding, let it first be clear that these people are not Christians who are abnormally good. It is not that they are individually better than others, and that therefore they are destined to receive greater glory. Please remember, overcomers are simply *normal* Christians. All others have become, for the moment, subnormal.

In past eternity God had a definite plan, a design which he has never abandoned. Overcomers are those who, having seen that design, have set themselves by God's grace to stand by it. They are *not* certain imaginary people who have gone further than Paul, or who take a different line from that revealed through Paul. They are, I repeat, no more than normal in God's eyes; they can claim no special credit.

Overcoming, in John's writings, does not mean simply the question of personal overcoming. It is not a matter of overcoming sin, which is better termed "deliverance," nor of personal holiness—the so-called "victorious life." The overcoming spoken of by John is the kind of overcoming that, in a given situation, lays claim to and holds that situation for God. In an hour when the Pauline message is rejected by so many, the Christian is tempted to say, "That is how things are. What can we do about it? We must just try to keep ourselves straight on certain lines, but we shall have to let some things pass as hopeless. They are beyond recovery. There is nothing we can do to improve them." Beset by circumstances, real and hypothetical, which we simply do not know how to contend with, it is easy to resign ourselves to the view that our particular situation is beyond recovery. There are too many things in it to be adjusted, too many painful steps to be taken in the outworking. The thing is impossible.

It is in such an hour that overcomers reassert, by their life and testimony, that God is not a man that he should change. His standards, they affirm, have not altered, and he has still set himself to have a heavenly City at the end, a heavenly Man today. What the whole Church, *as* the Church, ought to be doing but has left undone, they, representatively and *for* the Church, are raised up by God to do. Standing true to the victorious heavenly Man, they hold their ground. That is the "overcoming" spoken of here in the Word.

John in Revelation shows the sphere of the overcomers. It is within the defeated church today. Those of importance to God are those who now, each in his own situation, lay claim to those situations for God. There is a part of God's plan which concerns each of us, just where we are, and for it he needs overcomers. I say again, there is no special goodness about them; their only distinction is that they are not abnormally bad! They abide by God's standard, that is all. But knowing the Christian life, the heavenly calling of the Body, the warfare of the Church, they are like a lever in God's hands to dislodge Satan from his throne. They prepare themselves on the Church's behalf, and they fight for the Church. They put out all their effort, not for their own sakes but for the sake of the Body; and because they are ready, God sees the Church prepared as a bride. They set the torch as it were to the fire, and what the overcomers inherit the whole Church inherits.

YOU YOUNG MEN

Exodus, Leviticus, Numbers—these three books of the Old Testament offer an interesting parallel to Christian experience. I have likened them to the "sit," "walk," "stand" of Ephesians. (See Eph. 1:20; 4:1; 6:13.) Exodus sees Israel delivered from Egypt by a mighty hand, and established as the people of God through an irreversible work. Leviticus lays down the basis of their communion with him by blood, and their walk of holiness by the Cross. Numbers orders and arrays them for warfare, with a view to the enjoyment of their God-given inheritance. This last is stated clearly at the commencement of the book of Numbers, where, in Chapter 1:3, Aaron is told to number "all that are able to go forth to war in Israel."

Just prior to this statement, in the final chapter of Leviticus, it seems that the Lord sets out to assess which of his children are going to be of the greatest value to him. I refer to the instructions given there about voluntary vows (Lev.

27:1-8). We must distinguish carefully between this and the passage in Exodus 30 which speaks of the redemption money for their souls. That was commanded of every Israelite, and in every case it was exactly the same, namely, half a silver shekel. It speaks, I think, of what God is going to be *for us;* but here in Leviticus 27 it is a question of what we may be *for him,* and so this is expressed not as something commanded, but as a voluntary act. "When a man shall make a special vow, according to the estimation of persons unto the Lord, then thy estimation shall be ..." and there follows a scale of values in shekels, according to age and sex, which we may tabulate thus:

Age	For men	For women
Below 5 years	5 shekels	3 shekels
5-20 years	20 ''	10 ''
20-60 years	50 ''	30 ''
Over 60 years	15 ''	10 ''

God does not discount anybody, not even the children and babes, but we may ask ourselves: Why is there this high valuation on the over-twenty age group? Surely it is because, as we have just seen, the next book, Numbers, opens by defining those able to go forth to war as "from twenty years old and upward." This means, surely, that the value of our giving of ourselves, heart, mind, will and life to God is measured by him in terms of our fitness for war. On our part it is merely a vow—and God forbid that any of us should be vow-less Christians!—but on God's part it has definite values. Yes, it is good to save souls, good to have personal holiness, good to do a hundred-and-one useful things for God, but above all it is supremely precious to him that we be fit to take part in the age-long battle of the Lord, to dislodge his foes and to bring his people into the enjoyment of their inheritance in him. Jehovah is a man of war, and energy for war is what he prizes most highly.

The great Old Testament tragedy, of course, was that of the old men, when, in normal circumstances, their physical strength for war began to fail. But this is where we must at once come over in thought to the New Testament, for there, "though our outward man is decaying, yet our inward man is renewed day by day" (2 Cor. 4:16). The tree by the waterside does not wither. In a real Christian life there is no afternoon, no falling off of strength. Like that of Caleb, who was the true overcomer in the book of Numbers, our strength for war at eighty years can be as it was at forty, if we will wholly follow the Lord.

This is what I believe John is taking up and developing in his first Epistle, when he says: "I write unto you young men, because ye have overcome the evil one." Young men are naturally full of vigor, and this statement suggests once again the divine approval of their spiritual energy and of its fruits. But let us remember, John's classification of his readers into little children, young men, fathers, is not to be identified with that in Leviticus. He is talking to spiritual babes who already have assurance of forgiveness of sins, to spiritual warriors in whom God's Word abides, to spiritual fathers who carry along with them all they have gathered up as babes, children, men of war, into the full-ranged knowledge of him who is the very Origin of all things. Today no spiritual age group is excluded from a part in war. True, there should be no delayed maturity in the Christian life, just as there should be no retiring age in spiritual things. (And the term "young men" includes the young women, too, in the spiritual scale of military values, though in a sense this was already true in Leviticus.)

Whatever, then, be the length of our spiritual history, the question each of us must ask ourselves is: What will be my up-to-date value in the sanctuary? God has a definite estimate of how each of us counts for him. He knows us individually, and his sanctuary-value for every one is measured on the scale of spiritual strength. There is no need for any of us, whatever our years, to be written off at fifteen shekels when we can be priced as high as thirty or fifty. Oh, to drink today, every one of us, of Caleb's militant spirit!

THE ACCUSER OF THE BRETHREN

John wrote to his "little children" of the assurance of the forgiveness of sins. In one sense we are always, in John's term, little children, for in this life we never advance to a point where we have left behind our need for the precious Blood. It is indeed the very first weapon of the overcomer. Writing in Revelation 12 of the Accuser of the brethren "which accuseth them before our

God day and night," John tells us that "they overcame him because of the blood of the Lamb, and because of the word of their testimony, and they loved not their life even unto death" (verses 10, 11).

The basis of overcoming in the spiritual warfare is always the precious Blood. No one can ever get to the place where the Blood is not necessary. Satan is a murderer and a deceiver, he entices and he attacks, but today he specializes in accusing. In a very real sense he is the Accuser of the brethren, and it is here that our Lord meets him as Priest and Mediator. Heaven recognizes Satan's work and so must every Christian. Night and day he accuses us, and his accusation is directed at our conscience, which is the point where we most feel we lack the strength to fight him. His object is to drive us to think in despair. "Of what possible use am I to God?" Why are some Christians found from morning to night reproaching themselves and crying, "I am a hopeless failure. God can do nothing with me!"? It is because they have allowed themselves to accept the charges of the enemy as unanswerable. And if he can get us to this state, he is indeed the victor, for we have given the battle away. If, instead of looking at the glory of God, we only accept his accusations, and stop there, we are certainly left with no power to fight him.

Conscience is a very precious thing, but to repeat endlessly, "I am no good! I am no good!"—*that* is not Christian humility. It is healthy to confess our sins, but let us never carry confession to the point where, for us, our sinfulness looms larger than the work of Christ. The Devil knows there is no weapon more effective against the Christian than the creation of this illusion. What is the remedy? It is to say to the Lord, "Lord, I am no good!" but then to look away to his precious Blood, and to add: "But Lord, I am abiding in thee!"

Satan does not accuse without reason. There are, no doubt, plenty of sins to which he can point us; but the Blood of Jesus Christ cleanses us from all sin. Do we believe that? Then it is the answer to his charge. Sin calls for the Blood, but the Bible does not tell us that sin calls for accusation—not, that is to say, if we plead guilty. Of course, if we say we have no sin, John warns us that the door is then wide open to the Accuser. But if, standing in the light of God, we confess to him our guilt, then the Blood is powerful to cleanse, and all Satan's charges are rendered ineffective. Praise God for such an Advocate! Praise him for such a Priest! Let us never, never answer Satan either by boasting our good conduct or by bemoaning our sins, but always and only by the Blood. It is our wholly sufficient defense.

The precious Blood of Christ is our defense; the word of our testimony is our weapon of attack. By this is meant our testimony to man, but not to man alone. The victory of Christ, the fact that he reigns, that his Kingdom is near, that we have been translated from Satan's kingdom into his; all these are facts to be declared, not to men only, but to the powers of darkness. Affirm that God is King, that his Son is Victor, that Satan is defeated, that the kingdoms of this world are shortly to become the Kingdom of our God and of his Christ. These are positive divine facts, and they are our shafts of offense. Satan fears such declarations of spiritual fact. For the word of our testimony can move back the gates of hell. Declare that Jesus is Lord; that his Name is above every name. Declare it! *Say* it to the enemy. Many a time such testimony brings more results than does prayer.

Prayer has two sides: to God, and to the mountain. "Thou shalt say unto this mountain, be thou removed." We can say to Satan, "Leave this place!" Peter and John said to the paralytic man, "In the name of Jesus Christ of Nazareth, walk." They dealt directly with the case, where today we would probably have called a prayer meeting. Don't neglect prayer, but counting upon the efficacy of the precious Blood, speak also a word of testimony. Often times when we come to God, the atmosphere is oppressive and we cannot pray. What should we do? Don't give in, but taking God's Word, turn and speak to Satan. Declare the victory of the Lord. Declare that he has given us authority to tread on serpents and scorpions and over all the power of the enemy. And *then* pray!

Alas, we pay far too much attention today to the doctrine of the gospel, and far too little to the fact. And without the fact, we have no testimony. But Calvary is history. The gospel—the good news of this fact—is with us. For nearly two thousand years the fact of the gospel has been in the earth. The Lord has given us the precious

Blood, and a sure word of testimony. Let us face the enemy with these.

And finally these overcomers are men and women who know what it means to be nailed to the Cross—that is to say, to be "ruled out" altogether as men, so that whatever they accomplish, the glory is only his. We need not enlarge on this again here; but remember, it was Satan who challenged God concerning Job: "Skin for skin, yea, all that a man hath will he give for his life" (Job 2:4). But now, as if in answer to this, a great voice in heaven affirms concerning these who overcame: "They loved not their life even unto the death" (Rev. 12:11). Well could that same voice proclaim: "Now is come the salvation, and the power, and the kingdom of our God, and the authority of his Christ"!

"AND WHAT SHALL THIS MAN DO?"

We have spoken of some high matters, and lest we overreach ourselves I think it wise now to come briefly to something very practical, and to talk quite simply to my young brothers who desire to serve the Lord. In the last chapter of John's Gospel our Lord made a series of very personal challenges to his disciple Peter. Peter responded with some hesitation, and then we are told that at a point, as if to divert attention away from himself, he began to show a sudden interest in his fellow-fisherman, John. Looking round and seeing this "disciple whom Jesus loved" following, he said to Jesus: "Lord, and what shall this man do?"[1] But Jesus would not allow this switch of attention to someone else, and returned once more to the personal challenge to Peter himself: "What is that to thee? Follow thou me." What this incident says, it seems to me, is that no single one of us may evade the obligation to ask the same personal question of himself: "Lord, and what shall this man do?"—or in Paul's words: "What shall I do, Lord?" (Acts 22:10).

Some time ago, in England,[2] I was invited to meet a group of young men and women, most of whom were at that time preparing themselves to serve the Lord as missionaries in the East. They asked me if I would tell them what I regarded as the essential qualifications of a missionary. I replied that I indeed felt the days of missionaries are not over, and that God has called his servants of all nations to work alongside one another in the field. The notes that follow contain the essence of what I said to them then. They will be found to echo several of the matters we have treated at greater length already in these studies.

The Assurance of Salvation.

This is the starting-point, and experience warns us that it is never safe to take it for granted in making such a list of qualifications as this, or when addressing any group of men or women. The foundation of all service for the Lord is that we should have met him and come to know him for ourselves, and have received the absolute as-

---

[1] Literally, "Lord, and what of this man?"
[2] The time was 1938.

surance that, in him, we are eternally saved.

Christ Our Life.

We have to remind Christians today that many ancient religions of the East have a high ethical and moral code. In Chinese society, as in some others, while there may be less exacting standards on some matters, such things as anger and impatience in a man or woman are regarded as serious signs of lack of self-control. Yet missionaries who do not themselves know the victorious life of a Christian often display these things, and do not realize how much their testimony suffers as a consequence. Those to whom they are seeking to witness are, by this fact, given ground to regard themselves as religiously and morally superior. If we are to witness to Christ effectively among a people who already worship "self-mastery," and who even despise those who need recreation and comfort, it is necessary that in a real and convincing way we give proof by our lives of the true answer to "self." We must know the Cross as our deliverance from sin and the flesh, and find in Christ risen the sufficient power to walk in newness of life.

Entire Dependence on the Lord.

It is easy to exercise a "group faith"; it is much harder to trust God alone, and to do so without letting our eyes wander from him to the channel of supply. Westerners talk of "rice-Christians," but can we not recognize in all of us a sneaking tendency towards what, in more modern terms, we may call the "life of faith and hints," or as someone has shrewdly put it, "faith and postage-stamps"? It is quite wrong for God's servants to speak or write "on behalf of the work," and they must be very true with him about this. The less our hands touch the miracles of God in this way, the better. We should not be afraid to make things hard for God—so hard in fact that no one dare "join" unless he is called. Perhaps our surest safeguard is to concern ourselves with the needs of others. Care for them, and God will care for us.

A Specific Ministry.

As his children, we all of us have the general obligation of witnessing for the Lord, but the servant of God should go further than that. He should be marked by some special Spirit-wrought knowledge of God that is distinctively his own. Out of this should his ministry spring. We shall be of little use to the Church in China, or anywhere else for that matter, if all we can do is preach the gospel and edify in a general way. This is expected of every Christian, but Chinese believers will look in us for something more, something specific. Nor shall we satisfy their need with a special teaching or doctrine, however excellent, but only, I repeat, with a knowledge of the Lord that characterizes us because it is peculiarly our own. We complain sometimes that people are not hungry for the Word, but believe me, if we had something distinctive to give them, they would be. Are we, by our presence, creating in people a hunger for God? Food itself can create hunger if it is sufficiently appetizing, and people become hungry when they see men and women filled with the Spirit, full of love, not just preaching, or dispensing a general knowledge, but ministering spiritual riches that bear the marks of personal dealings with him. Yes, there is something wrong with us if we are not hunger-creators.

The Atttitude of a Learner.

Always travel with a large "L" on your back![3] Those who set out to be "teachers" of others put themselves in a dangerous position. Many overstretch themselves, and by talking about things they have not put to the test of experience, create problems in the minds of simple saints. If we are oversure, and ready enough to say something hastily, we put ourselves under the necessity of remembering next time what answer we gave, or we may discover we have now given a different one! The more we profess to know, the more room there will be for our hearers to criticize, because they will be led to expect more of us. It is such superiority, born of the overconfidence that we *know*, that imperceptibly but surely closes the door to what we may indeed have been given to share with others. Rather do we need grace to admit our ignorance, and to ask the Lord about it. We must be willing to say, "I do not know." People will not be hard on the

[3]At the time when this talk was given, the "L" plate on the cars of those driving with a Learner's Licence had not long been introduced in Britain, and the idea of thus publicly proclaiming oneself to be a "learner" appealed strongly to the author.—Ed.

worker who adopts the attitude: "If you have something to say, I am willing to listen, because I too am a disciple of the Lord." My counsel to you therefore is to remain for very long a learner. Keep that "L" on your back for at least ten years!

A History of the Acts of God.

I believe, further, that every servant of God should have some things in his history which are an abiding proof of the presence and power of God with him. I have given an account elsewhere of an incident where God answered the prayer of faith for rain in a quite miraculous way that none of us who were present ever forgot.[4] But Western missionaries have a background. There are certain things for which they have worked out an explanation, and Christian teachers are ready enough today to excuse doctrinally the comparative infrequency of miracles in our time. Such excuses will never be accepted by simple believers, for often enough they have seen the hand of God at work themselves.

I remember one such, Chen the tailor. He was indeed very simple. Moreover he had never met another Christian. All he had was a copy of Mark's Gospel, but through reading it he had met the Savior, and he had believed. Then he came to Chapter 16—the so-called "doubtful passage"!—and after reading it carefully he said to the Lord, "Lord, I am so small that one small gift will suffice me. Give me the gift of healing!" At once he went out, and going from house to house, prayed for the sick in his village. When

[4]*Sit, Walk, Stand,* Chapter 3.

later we met him and questioned him closely, it became quite evident that his humility, together with his absolute trust in God quite regardless of the gravity of the diseases he tackled or of any immediate evidence of an answer, had in fact led to some wonderful happenings in that village. Idolators had been convinced of the Lord's superiority to heathen gods, and some had believed. Yet we found him still just a humble brother, making no extravagant claims, and quietly continuing to witness to the Lord Jesus as he pursued his employment as a simple village tailor.

I confess that, on one occasion in the West, when I was attending a conference of very sincere brethren and heard them become more and more deeply involved in discussion of some difficult doctrinal question, I was at length impelled to break in. "My dear brothers!" I exclaimed. "In my country, all your knowledge of these nice Scriptural details would avail you nothing if, when the need arose, you did not know how to cast out demons!" Today we have become civilized, and as a result, we often close the door to God. It sometimes seems to me that God brings us up to a certain point of opportunity, and then, because our natural caution forbids us to step out in faith on him, instead of a miracle of life, all we get is a new teaching. But surely, we must *expect* God to seal his Word with signs and wonders. If we truly know God, his wondrous acts cannot be far away. And today Satan's seat is to be challenged by our faith in a living God.

THE CALLING OF GOD

No master has so many servants as our Master, and for each he has a suitable employment. For Joseph he had a particular task, to save Israel from famine. Samuel came at the hour chosen, for the very special work of setting aside the priest in favor of the king, even as later Elijah came to set aside the king for the prophet. The little maid was at hand to testify to Naaman in his need. Even an ass was ready for Jesus to ride into Jerusalem.

Many murmur against the position God has given them, or against the task he has entrusted to them in the Body. They want to do this, but God puts them into that. They have an ambition to serve him here, but his plan for them lies somewhere else. When faced by such apparent reverses, it is well to remember that the purpose of God for us in his Church goes back before our conversion, for his foreknowledge has prepared our circumstances and determined our way even before we were born. Isaiah was chosen from birth, Saul of Tarsus "from the womb," Jeremiah still earlier, before he was formed in the womb. True the case of Saul puzzled Ananias, in view of what he had heard from others of this "chosen vessel"! But the whole road is wonderfully prepared for his servants by God. He determines whose child we shall be, though sometimes we may think we have been born into the wrong family! Some of us approve of our parents, but would like perhaps to change our brothers and sisters, or our other relatives! But Joseph said:

"God sent me before you to preserve life." If we have not seen God's hand in his choices, we have lost a great opportunity to bring him praise.

David's work began with Goliath, but already he had learned the lesson in his shepherd days. "Jehovah delivered me out of the paw of the lion," he could say. Peter was a fisherman, familiar with the dragnet. Perhaps for this reason he could better understand the "great sheet" at Joppa. Paul found Aquila and Priscilla through his ability to make tents. There was no need for someone without that trade to acquire it in order to help these two to become, as they did, careful exponents of the way of God. And in a time of declension in Ephesus, a Timothy was at hand who from a babe had known the sacred writings.

God never does a thing suddenly; he has always prepared long, long before. So there is nothing to murmur about, nothing to be proud of, in the calling of God. There is also no one of whom to be jealous, for other people's advantages have nothing to do with us. "It is not of him that willeth, nor of him that runneth, but of God that hath mercy" (Rom. 9:16). Our heritage, our birth, our natural equipment; these are things already determined by God. We may pick up other things on the way, for we are always learning; but the way is his way. When we look back over our life, we bow and acknowledge that all was prepared by God. There is no need to fear we have missed something. To have such an attitude of heart, *that* is true rest.

God is a God who works, and he started many years ago. When he wants a special kind of servant, or when the Church needs a special kind of help, God is not unprepared. He never encounters an emergency. In the history of his children, his hand is everywhere. Each of us would say, if we pondered a minute, "All my life his grace has followed me." The words of Paul, though used, it is true, in another connection, effectively summarize such an attitude to the providence of God: "Let each man abide in that calling wherein he was called" (1 Cor. 7:20). When we see the purpose of God, such words as these can take on a large meaning. God has called each of us, and is preparing us, for tasks foreknown to him. "I press on," Paul says elsewhere, "if so be that I may apprehend *that for which also I was apprehended* by Christ Jesus."

THE SPIRIT OF TRUTH

Finally, I would say a little more about the work of the Holy Spirit. In earlier chapters, especially when discussing the ministry of Paul, we have spoken frequently of the need for a revelation of divine things. More than once have we said that it is essential to *see* the purpose of God, to *see* the Person and work of Christ, to *see* the Church, the Body of Christ. To this some reader may be goaded to reply, concerning one or other of these things: "I *don't* see that. What do you suggest that I do?"

For answer I could point once more to the Spirit of truth, recalling again that he is a Person, close at hand—nay, dwelling now within our hearts—ready to help each one of us in our need.

It is the apostle John who tells us how, at a time of great mystification for the disciples, Jesus assured them of the Holy Spirit's coming, to bear witness of himself, and to guide them into all the truth.

Whether it be for the initial revelation to our hearts of divine things, or amid the discipline that must follow ere those divine things become truly a part of us, we shall find it necessary to turn again and again to this gracious Helper of our infirmities. It is by his revelation alone that we behold spiritual realities; it is by his loving discipline that we enter into those realities. By the former, he opens the gateway to progress; by the latter, he leads us on in the pathway of progress. The former is the foundation, the latter the superstructure. Without revelation by the Spirit we cannot commence the course, but without the discipline of the Spirit we cannot complete it. Both these aspects of the Spirit's work are equally essential, but for both we can assuredly count upon him.

The Father has conceived a plan; the Son has carried it out; now it is the Spirit who communicates to us what the Son has accomplished for us. We readily acknowledge the completeness of the work of the Son, when he said, "It is finished," and sat down at the right hand of the Majesty on high. But if we do not doubt that the Son has perfected the work committed to him by the Father, why then do we doubt that the Spirit will perfect the work committed to him by the Son?

The work of the Son is as comprehensive as

the work of the Father. It does not go one whit
beyond it, but nor does it fall one whit short of it.
As great as is the work of the Father, so great is
the work of the Son; and as great as is the work of
the Son, so great is the work of the Spirit. There
is not one particle of the work completed by the
Son for us that will not be completed by the
Spirit in us. All the fullness of spiritual reality
that is in Christ will be imparted to us by the
Spirit of Christ. Of himself, Jesus said, "I am the
Reality," and of the Spirit, "He shall guide you
into all Reality." The question of coming into all
the fullness of spiritual reality rests, therefore,
not with us but with the Spirit. It is not a question of our capacity, or of our ability, but of the
absolute faithfulness of the Holy Spirit of God.
Can he be depended on to do all the work committed to him by the Son? We must learn to trust
him. We must learn to count upon his twofold
work, first of revealing to us the nature and the
dimensions of divine reality and secondly of
bringing us into every whit of the reality he has
revealed.

As we look around us, we cannot fail to observe a tragic lack in the experience of so many
Christians. There is nothing about their lives to
indicate fullness. They have not sufficient for
their own needs, much less have they anything
to spare for others. Why are they so poor? Is it
not because they do not know the discipline of
the Spirit? The Psalmist says, "In pressure thou
hast enlarged me" (Psalm 4:1[5]). The object of all

---

[5]J. N. Darby, *New Translation.*

pressure is enlargement. James says something similar in his Epistle: "Did not God choose them that are poor as to the world to be rich in faith?" (James 2:5). The object of temporal poverty is eternal enrichment. God never intended that pressure and poverty should issue in nothing. His purpose is that all pressure should lead to enlargement, all poverty to enrichment. God's goal for his people is neither continuous straitness nor continuous poverty. For straitness and poverty are never the end; they are only the means to God's end. Straitness is the pathway to expansion, poverty the pathway to wealth.

Read again Revelation chapter 21. What a picture you get there of fullness! You may spend much time on the book of Revelation and still understand little of its meaning, but you surely cannot fail to understand this, that chapter 21 speaks of a wealth, an abundance, a glory, that this earth has never yet known, no, not even in the fabulous days of Solomon. When were the streets of earth ever paved with gold? When had this world no need of the sun to light it? What riches! What splendor! Never was earthly empire so wealthy or so radiant as New Jerusalem. And what breadth! Never was city seen on earth one hundredth part of the scale of this. And he that overcometh, we are told, shall inherit these things!

Some have asked why, in the new heavens and the new earth, we read of God and of the Lamb, but find there no mention of the Holy Spirit. Surely the answer is that just as, today, Christ has finished his work, and the outcome of that work of Christ is seen in the Church, so, in that day, the Holy Spirit will have finished *his* work, and the outcome of that work of the Spirit will be seen in the New Jerusalem. For all that is there is real—the full realization by the Spirit of what he came to do. When you touch the Church today, you touch Christ, but it will be no less true that, when you touch the City then, you touch the Spirit of Christ. There the Church will be filled with the Spirit of God in his sevenfold fullness; there, as the City, she will manifest in herself the Spirit's work in completeness, for she will be holy, as her Lord.

But how does the Church reach that goal? Only by traveling the pathway from pressure to enlargement, from poverty to enrichment. You ask: What do we mean by enlargement through pressure? When three are shut into a furnace and the three become four, that is enlargement through pressure. Some find a furnace rather close quarters for three, so they seek a way of escape; others accept the limitation, and in accepting it, make room for a Fourth. Not to let difficulties shut us out from God, but to let them shut us in to him, that is enlargement through pressure. For Paul and Silas, the prison gates could only shut the world out and shut God in; so their prison, instead of cramping them, released them into greater fullness. God let trial upon trial press upon Job, but his trials only pressed him to God's goal. To John, in the island for the testimony, the risen Lord himself opened the door and showed him the glorious consummation of all things. Some, through pressure, reach God's end; others come to an end in the pressure. Some die in straitness; others, through straitness, find fullness of life. Some murmur when trials befall them, and find in them only limitation, restriction and death; others praise God in the trials, and find in them the pathway to enlargement, liberation and abundance of life.

Many Christians are so poor that they have not even sufficient to meet their own needs. Alas for any who go to them for help! Other Christians are so rich you can never assess their wealth. You can never meet a difficulty they have not met; you can never find yourself in a situation where they are unable to help. They have abundant resources to meet the demands of all who go to them in need. Many Christians do not go utterly bankrupt simply because they are being ministered to by others, who continually pour their wealth into the Body. Such Christians little know how much they owe to other believers, some of whom they might even be tempted to despise. It may be that, when a friend comes from a journey and expects bread from us, the Lord will permit us to turn to a neighbor for something to give him; but it may be that he will say to us, "Give ye them to eat."

Spiritual poverty and spiritual straitness are two of the greatest problems in the Church, but poverty is effect, not cause, and straitness is effect, not cause. The cause of poverty and the cause of straitness is lack of the Spirit's discipline. Those who are wealthy and those who are enlarged are they, and they only, who have experienced such discipline. They have been through deep waters, and have a spiritual history with God, because they have suffered for the Body's sake. Their sicknesses, their domestic problems, their adversities—all were for the increase of Christ in his people. Those, on the other hand, who bypass such disciplines, choosing instead a life of ease and comfort in a pathway of prosperity—they are the straitened and the poverty-stricken. The poor and needy come to them in vain for help. They have no overflow.

Do you think preaching is just preaching? Do you think ministry is just ministry? Believe me, they are not. Serving God is not just a matter of words or works, but of how much you have been through. If the Spirit is never allowed to trouble you, you will be condemned to poverty all your life. You will never learn how blessed it is to draw fullness from the Lord, not for yourself, but for others. And *that* is ministry.

Revelation waits upon discipline. It is our acceptance of the discipline of the Spirit that opens the way for him to reveal to us the realities that are in Christ, and to bring us into these. Avoidance of that discipline denies him the opportunity of doing so. Every day God is looking for opportunities to enlarge us, but when difficulties arise we avoid them, when trials come we circumvent them. Oh, but at what loss to ourselves! And at what loss to God's people! Of course there is no way of dodging divine chastening that comes to us when we have deliberately moved out of the will of the Lord; that is something different, designed for our correction and cure. We cannot escape that, but we can, if we will, dodge the creative disciplines of the Spirit. If however we are willing to commit ourselves to his dealings, he will take us in hand and bring us to God's goal. Are we willing to say, "Lord, I will drink the cup thou givest to its last dregs; I will bear the cross, and seek no relief in gall or vinegar"? Oh, for an utter consecration in his people, that will enable God to do all that in his heart he has planned for them! That will lead to fullness, the fullness of the New Jerusalem. There is not one nugget of gold in that City but has been tried in the furnace; not a precious stone but has been passed through the fires; not a pearl but has been produced through suffering.

When Peter put to Jesus his question about John, what was our Lord's reply? "If I will that he tarry till I come, what is that to thee?" *Till I come!* The ministry of the Spirit of truth set forth by John will go on until the story is completed; nothing can stop it. The purpose of God in his Church is going to be accomplished; it can never be thwarted. The vision of the Holy City, made ready as a bride adorned for her husband, will unfailingly come to pass, and we shall see it. No one can touch that "till I come"; it is settled in heaven.

Shall we not, therefore, put ourselves into our Father's safe hands, that he may order our lives as he wills? It will be his care to see that the transforming work of the Holy Spirit within us is no less perfect, no less sure, than was the redemption first accomplished on our behalf by his beloved Son.